Karen Martini

Karen Martini
Cooking at home

Photography by Earl Carter

LANTERN

an imprint of

PENGUIN BOOKS

Contents

At home

The recipes in this book are a fair reflection of what has been going on in my household during the last two to three years. The food I cook is still very much the result of my heritage, hunger and curiosity – as I said in my first book, *Where the Heart Is*. These days, however, I find organisation is as important as inspiration when it comes to creating new dishes.

The biggest change in my life has come with the arrival of my daughter, Stella, in 2006. I no longer have time for much leisurely contemplation. Instead, I scribble my ideas in point form on the backs of dockets, tiny scraps of paper or the upper left-hand corner of my diary. Shopping, once a casual cruise of the market or supermarket aisle, is now a precise journey, usually involving a list or two.

As in most households, the end of each day brings the almighty question of what to have for dinner. On a good day, I have my strategy mapped out; on a not-so-good day, I might have six marylands of duck defrosting in the sink, waiting for me to transform them into a new dish – which may or may not hit the table by 10.30 p.m. – to be eaten by my very hungry and long-suffering husband, Michael.

Cooking at home and eating in most nights has helped me to understand how much thought and effort is required to come up with something different for dinner, day in and day out. I have a massive repertoire of recipes, yet I still struggle to produce food that is varied. Like most people, I am tempted to stick to my favourites – those dishes I know I can whip up without fuss. I do always try to experiment, even just a little. I'll make the bolognese sauce I have been making for years, but may use, say, veal and pork sausage instead of beef mince to keep things interesting.

This is the feedback I get constantly from readers and viewers. Most stress the need for simplicity – no one wants to have to rifle through cupboards looking for sixteen pieces of equipment to make a meal that needs thirty exotic ingredients. But people are also interested in variety, in how to add that twist to please the eye and surprise the palate. The recipes in this book – recipes I have cooked for friends and family over the last twelve years – are all about

taking familiar food and making it special. Chargrilled tuna is given new life when served with smoky eggplant; the humble omelette becomes a gourmet feast with the addition of crab and corn; an old-fashioned cheesecake takes on a different character when paired with wine-soaked berries.

How to entertain is always a topic of conversation. I am probably typical of most people in my desire to keep the fuss to a minimum so as to spend more time with my guests. These days, with a small child on the move and another on the way, I opt for grazing, particularly in hot weather. We invite people over and offer food straight off the barbecue, served with salads, breads and cheeses – it's a very casual affair. Again, we stick to the favourites, but add a little something extra: some herb butter to enliven a nice piece of Scotch fillet, a tuna salad pepped up with some paprika.

One of the big changes in my approach to food of late has been my concern for produce. Like many others, I want to know how long a particular item has been in transit and how it was treated on the journey. There's so much choice out there.

While most of us occasionally grab a few vegies at the supermarket, I'd like to think that more and more people are heading for their local greengrocer, or to the farmers' markets that are springing up all over the place. We are learning the value of absolute freshness and gaining a true appreciation of organic produce.

Cooking for a family reminds me of my own childhood. My mum never made packet cakes, and was bemused if we brought them home from friends' houses. Baking was a big part of life in our house, as was the Sunday roast. My mother was a very good cook, but she was not adventurous. She'd say, 'Oh no, we won't be using any of that coriander.' But now she grows fresh herbs in her garden, and is always asking for ideas on how to cook with them. I think she is typical of many Australians who are coming to understand how just one extra ingredient can turn a fairly ordinary dish into a special meal.

Mum taught me one of the most important things I know about food: sharing a meal with people you care about is what matters most. The table was always set, with the cloth, the bread, the water. Everything was ready so we could sit down to eat and chat about our respective days. It would be wonderful to preserve these household traditions, and if this collection of recipes does nothing else, I would like to think it encourages people – family, friends, households – to share at least one meal together, two or three times a week. So simple, but truly one of life's greatest pleasures.

Dry + Bread

rye \ pane du casa

Baguette \ Batard \ ciabatta

✱ pickled onions

✱ sea salt flakes

green olives

anchovies

white marinated anchovies

dried chilli flakes -   chick peas

dried mint   tinned tuna

black pepper corns -   lebanese bread

frozen peas   Cannellini beans

Canola oil   longrain rice

rocket salt   ground corriander

Tahini   cracked wheat

blanched Almonds - Cinnamon

cumin seeds   sticks

sweet pumpkin -   Dukka

fried shallots -

pinenuts -

Sumac .

pomegranate molasses

rosewater

Deli x Cheese + Dairy

aged goats cheese

ricotta (x 2 pkt)

2 x filo pastry

3 x dozen eggs

butter \ milk

Sour cream -

3 x cream   provolone

sliced pancette chilli

Halumi cheese

black olives

goats curd

leg ham \ chorizo

yoghurt

Green olive tapenade

Liven up an antipasto platter with bruschetta spread generously with this tapenade. Alternatively, serve it with grilled lamb cutlets, or toss it through long pasta with toasted almonds and parsley, and top with freshly grated parmesan.

Squeeze the garlic flesh from the bulb and place in a food processor. Add the olives, capers, anchovies, garlic, chilli flakes and parsley and process until well combined. Add the olive oil and process until smooth. Transfer to an airtight jar and store in the fridge for up to 7 days.

Makes about 1⅓ cups

1 bulb garlic, roasted at 160°C for 40 minutes
125 g green olives, pitted and chopped
2 tablespoons capers
4 anchovy fillets, chopped
½ clove garlic, chopped
1 teaspoon dried chilli flakes
2 sprigs flat-leaf parsley
125 ml extra virgin olive oil

> Puff pastry tart with sardines and green olive tapenade

This is my version of pissaladière, a French tart made with caramelised onions. The sardines and salty olive paste are a great match for the sweetness of the onions. Perfect for a light lunch or starter with a salad of simply dressed leaves.

Heat the olive oil in a large frying pan over low heat, add the onion, thyme, salt and pepper and cook, stirring frequently, for about 30 minutes or until golden brown and caramelised.

Preheat the oven to 220°C. Line a baking tray with baking paper.

Cut a 40 cm × 20 cm rectangle from the pastry sheet and place on the baking tray. Spoon on the caramelised onion and top with the sardines. Roll-pinch the edges in 2–3 cm, then bake for 12–15 minutes or until the pastry is cooked.

Just before serving, drizzle lemon juice over the tart, top with dollops of olive tapenade and scatter with parsley leaves.

Serves 6–8

100 ml extra virgin olive oil
5 brown onions, finely sliced
3 sprigs thyme
sea salt and freshly ground black pepper
500 g frozen puff pastry, defrosted
14 fresh sardine fillets
½ lemon, juiced
1½ tablespoons green olive tapenade (see left)
12 large parsley leaves

< Goat's cheese toasts with grilled asparagus salad

The simple combination of aged goat's cheese melted on crusty bread served with dressed leaves is a culinary delight not to be missed.

Preheat a chargrill or barbecue plate to medium. Cook the asparagus for 4–5 minutes, then slice into shards on an angle.

To make the dressing, crush the garlic, salt and basil leaves in a mortar and pestle. Add the oil and pound to a paste. Season with pepper and set aside.

Toast the bread under a hot grill or in the oven until golden, then top with goat's cheese. Place under a hot grill or in the oven for 4–5 minutes, until the cheese starts to melt.

Arrange the radicchio on serving plates and scatter with the rocket, onion, asparagus and basil leaves. Sit the toasts on top, drizzle with lemon juice and basil dressing and season to taste with pepper.

Serves 4

1 bunch asparagus, trimmed
8 slices sourdough baguette, sliced on an angle
200 g aged goat's cheese, sliced
½ head radicchio, shredded
2 handfuls rocket leaves
6 pickled onions, cut into fine wedges
5 basil leaves, torn
1 tablespoon lemon juice
freshly ground black pepper

Basil dressing
½ clove garlic
sea salt
15 basil leaves
2½ tablespoons extra virgin olive oil
freshly ground black pepper

Tarator

Tarator is a Turkish nut sauce that is delicious with crusty bread. It is also scrumptious with grilled poultry or seafood and it adds texture to the simplest grilled or roasted meat or fish. If you like, substitute almonds for the walnuts.

Place the walnuts in a medium saucepan and cover with water. Bring to the boil over medium heat and simmer for 30 minutes. Drain well.

Transfer the walnuts to a food processor, add the garlic and process until combined. Add the bread and process. Add the vinegar, baharat, lemon juice, water and olive oil, season with salt and pepper and process until the mixture forms a rough paste (or until smooth if you prefer). Stir in the chopped mint.

To serve, sprinkle with mint leaves and drizzle with olive oil, if using.

Makes about 2 cups

150 g walnuts
2 cloves garlic
1 slice stale bread
3 tablespoons red wine vinegar
½ pinch baharat (see glossary)
½ lemon, juiced
200 ml water
100 ml extra virgin olive oil
sea salt and freshly ground black pepper
6 sprigs mint, coarsely chopped
mint leaves, to serve (optional)
olive oil, to serve (optional)

Ricotta pastries with mint and peas

Little and big kids alike will adore these pastries. I've used mint in this recipe but basil, oregano or dill would work just as well. You can freeze the pastries and have them on hand when catering for large groups.

Preheat the oven to 200°C. Place the ricotta, egg yolks, peas, fresh and dried mint, salt and pepper in a medium bowl and stir to combine.

Spread out the pastry sheets and cut each one into four strips lengthways. Place two strips of pastry on a large cutting board, brush lightly with butter and put another two strips on top. Repeat once more to make three layers on each strip. Place 1 tablespoon ricotta mixture on the end of each strip and fold the pastry over to form a triangle. Keep folding all the way up the strip to form two sealed triangles. Brush a little egg white on the ends of the pastry to seal. Repeat with the remaining pastry strips and ricotta mixture to make about 20 triangles.

Arrange the triangles on a non-stick baking tray, brush with the remaining butter and bake for 15–20 minutes or until golden.

Spread the tzatziki on a plate and place the pastries on top. Sprinkle with sumac, if using.

Makes about 20

350 g ricotta
2 free-range eggs, separated
½ cup frozen peas, blanched and drained
20 mint leaves, chopped
1½ tablespoons dried mint
sea salt and freshly ground black pepper
375 g filo pastry
150 g unsalted butter, melted
200 g ready-made tzatziki
sumac, to serve (optional; see glossary)

> King prawns with chilli and oregano

Serve these little morsels as robust finger food or pile them high for a buffet-style feast. They'll be snapped up fast. Make sure you have plenty of napkins nearby.

Preheat the oven to 220°C or preheat the grill to high. Cut the prawns in half lengthways, leaving the head and tail intact, and devein with a small sharp knife or scissors. Place on a baking tray, season with salt and pepper and drizzle with a little olive oil.

Combine the chilli, garlic, oregano, parsley, lemon zest and remaining olive oil in a food processor or blender, season well and process to a paste.

Bake or grill the prawns for 6–7 minutes or until they just change colour. Transfer to a large serving platter and top with herb paste. Serve with lemon wedges and snow pea shoots.

Makes 16

16 very large green (raw) king prawns (shrimp)
sea salt and freshly ground black pepper
150 ml extra virgin olive oil
1–2 small red chillies, chopped
1 clove garlic, sliced
1 bunch oregano, leaves only
½ bunch flat-leaf parsley, leaves only
2 teaspoons finely grated lemon zest
lemon wedges and snow pea (mange-tout) shoots,
   to serve

Baked ricotta slices with grapes, olives and oregano

The combination of grapes and olives baked on the ricotta is unusual, but delicious – trust me. You can buy packaged ricotta from most supermarkets but it has a much better flavour and texture when it's bought fresh from a deli or specialty cheese shop.

Preheat the oven to 210°C. Pour 3 tablespoons olive oil into a large ovenproof dish and place the sliced ricotta in the base. Season with salt and pepper.

Toss the grapes in 1 tablespoon olive oil and scatter over the ricotta. Top with the olives and herbs and sprinkle with chilli flakes.

Drizzle with the remaining olive oil and bake for about 25 minutes or until the ricotta is firm and golden around the edges. Serve at room temperature with crusty bread.

Serves 6–8

125 ml extra virgin olive oil
400 g ricotta, well drained and
    cut into 3 cm thick slices
sea salt and freshly ground black pepper
150 g seedless green grapes, sliced into rounds
50 g manzanilla olives, pitted
¼ bunch oregano, leaves only
8 sprigs thyme
½ teaspoon dried chilli flakes, or to taste
crusty bread, to serve

Filo pastry tarts with smoked trout
and crisp pancetta (see page 16)

Filo pastry tarts with smoked trout and crisp pancetta

These tarts make a great starter, breakfast or light lunch with a watercress salad, and are quick to make, with no fiddly blind baking or pastry resting. Smoked trout and crispy pancetta is a particularly delicious combination. You could also use bacon. Recipe pictured previous page.

Preheat the oven to 220°C. Cut the pastry sheets into 50 squares approximately 15–18 cm each, then cover with a damp tea towel so the pastry doesn't dry out. Brush ten 12 cm ovenproof dishes generously with melted butter and place a square of filo in each. Brush each filo square with melted butter and repeat until there are five layers of pastry in each dish.

Scatter the trout and pancetta among the dishes, then top with the chives, tarragon and green onion.

Place the eggs and cream in a large bowl and whisk well. Season with salt and pepper, then pour the cream mixture evenly into the dishes.

Bake for 10–15 minutes or until the pastry is golden and the filling is cooked. Serve with lemon wedges and curly endive, if using. To add a decadent touch, spoon a little salmon caviar onto the tarts just before serving.

Makes 10

375 g filo pastry
melted butter, for brushing
1 smoked trout, skin and bones removed, flaked
10 slices pancetta (see glossary), crisped in the oven
  for 5–6 minutes
½ bunch chives, chopped
2 sprigs tarragon, chopped
5 green onions, sliced
6 free-range eggs
500 ml pouring cream
sea salt and freshly ground black pepper
lemon wedges and curly endive (optional), to serve
salmon caviar (optional), to serve

> Kipfler skins with tahini sour cream

These 'chips' are to die for – the secret is in the double cooking. After their first cooking, they can be kept in the fridge for a couple of days. They are scrumptious with flathead fillets in beer batter (see page 109).

Preheat the oven to 220°C. Scatter rock salt evenly over a baking tray, then place the potatoes on top and prick with a fork. Bake for 30–40 minutes or until tender.

When cool enough to handle, cut them into quarters lengthways.

Place the potatoes on a clean baking tray, drizzle with olive oil and roast for 20–25 minutes or until golden and crisp. Remove and season with salt. (Alternatively, shallow-fry the potatoes over medium–high heat until golden, then drain on paper towels.)

Combine the sour cream, tahini and yoghurt in a small bowl and serve with the potato skins.

Serves 6

2 cups rock salt
10 large kipfler potatoes
100 ml extra virgin olive oil
sea salt
½ cup sour cream
1½ tablespoons tahini (see glossary)
½ cup plain yoghurt

Spanish white anchovies on bruschetta with fennel and cucumber pickle

Available from specialist delis, Spanish white anchovies are delicious and taste completely different from the standard anchovies. These tasty little morsels are a fun way to entertain and make it easy for you to join the party. The quick pickle will keep in the fridge for a couple of days and is delicious chopped finely and sprinkled over salads or wherever pickles are required.

To make the pickle, combine the fennel, cucumber, shallots and green chilli in a medium bowl. Place the vinegar, garlic, salt, sugar, red chilli, mustard seeds and oil in a small saucepan and bring to the boil. Pour the hot liquid over the vegetables, toss gently and set aside for about 10 minutes.

Arrange the toasted sourdough on a serving platter, then top with anchovies and crumbled fetta. Serve with the pickle.

Makes 12 pieces

12 slices sourdough baguette, cut on an angle, rubbed with garlic, drizzled with olive oil and toasted
250 g Spanish white marinated anchovies
50 g soft marinated fetta

Fennel and cucumber pickle

1 small bulb fennel, trimmed and cut into rounds
1 Lebanese cucumber, sliced lengthways
2 golden shallots, thickly sliced
1 green chilli, sliced
120 ml white wine vinegar
1 clove garlic, crushed
1 tablespoon salt flakes
2 tablespoons sugar
½ red chilli, split
1 tablespoon mustard seeds
100 ml extra virgin olive oil

Bruschetta with bruised tomatoes, mozzarella and basil oil

This is very much a 'less is more' dish, and the quality of the ingredients is crucial. It's worth searching for vine-ripened tomatoes, a fruity olive oil and the freshest basil. And don't skip the step of squashing the tomato into the bread – this is what makes it authentic.

Place 14 of the largest basil leaves in a mortar and pestle or food processor with 1 clove garlic, some salt and 2 tablespoons olive oil. Grind or process to a paste.

Combine the yoghurt and 1 tablespoon olive oil in a small bowl, add the mozzarella and mix well.

Toast the bread on both sides under a hot grill or in a toaster until golden. Rub with the remaining garlic clove, brush with the remaining oil and top with the tomato, gently squashing the tomato pieces into the bread with the back of a spoon. Top with the mozzarella mixture.

Fold the remaining basil leaves through the paste mixture and spoon over the bruschetta. Season with salt and pepper, cut in half on the diagonal and serve immediately.

Serves 6

20 large basil leaves
2 cloves garlic
sea salt and freshly ground black pepper
150 ml extra virgin olive oil
2 tablespoons plain yoghurt
1 ball Italian buffalo mozzarella or 4 bocconcini,
   cut into chunks
6 thick slices sourdough bread
4 very ripe tomatoes, cut into chunks

> Kingfish and smoked trout rillettes

Essentially a smoked fish pâté, this dish should be served at room temperature – it tastes so much better. You can also spread it on crostini, roll it in a white bread pin roll or shape it into quenelles and serve with an avocado, lemon and asparagus salad.

Fill a medium frying pan with lightly salted water and bring to the boil over medium heat. Add the kingfish and simmer for 1 minute. Remove the pan from the heat and set aside for 6–8 minutes. Remove the fillets from the pan and place in a colander. Cover with plastic film and set aside.

Place the butter and yoghurt in a large bowl and whisk well. Add the egg yolks, olive oil, salt and pepper and whisk to a smooth, glossy paste. Don't worry if the mixture splits – just keep whisking and warm gently over a pan of simmering water and it will come back together.

Flake the kingfish and trout into a medium bowl. Allow the fish to cool to room temperature, then add to the butter mixture, along with the lemon juice and chives. Fold gently to combine and check the seasoning.

Line a glass bowl with lemon slices, then spoon the rillettes into the bowl. Serve with toasted baguette slices.

Makes enough for 20–25 toasts

400 g kingfish fillets, skin removed
100 g unsalted butter, softened
4 tablespoons plain yoghurt
2 free-range egg yolks
2 tablespoons extra virgin olive oil
sea salt and freshly ground black pepper
150 g smoked trout, skin and bones removed
1 lemon, juiced
½ bunch chives, finely chopped
1 lemon, extra, very finely sliced
thin slices baguette, drizzled with olive oil
   and toasted, to serve

Spanish-inspired spiced almonds

These nuts, coated with a garlic and spice mix, are highly addictive and great with drinks – they beat any store-bought ones hands down. Served with chilled dry sherry, the spicy combination really gets the palate going.

Preheat the oven to 170°C and line a baking tray with baking paper. Melt the butter and olive oil in a large frying pan over medium heat. Add the almonds and garlic and stir constantly for 4–5 minutes or until golden brown. Drain on paper towels, discard the garlic and place the almonds in a large bowl.

Place the salt and coriander seeds in a mortar and pestle and grind to a powder. Add the sugar and spices and mix well. Add the spice mix and egg white to the almonds and toss together.

Spread on the baking tray and toast in the oven for 5 minutes. Remove and cool completely on the tray, then store in an airtight container for up to a week until ready to serve.

Serves 6

40 g unsalted butter
3 tablespoons extra virgin olive oil
400 g large blanched almonds
3 large cloves garlic, bruised with the back of a knife
4 tablespoons sea salt flakes
1 tablespoon coriander seeds
2 teaspoons castor sugar
2 teaspoons ground cumin
1 teaspoon dried chilli flakes
1 teaspoon smoked paprika
1 teaspoon sweet paprika
2 pinches of cayenne pepper
½ egg white, lightly whisked

Vol au vents with quail eggs

You can make your own vol au vents but most specialty food stores and bakeries sell miniature ones, which saves time. For a sleek effect, serve the vol au vents on a dark platter. And if you can afford it, use real caviar in place of the lumpfish roe.

Place the quail eggs in a saucepan and cover with cold water. Bring to the boil over medium heat and simmer for 5 minutes. Remove the eggs and place in a bowl of cold water, then peel carefully.

Spoon or pipe a little mayonnaise into each vol au vent case. Place a sprig of endive on the mayonnaise and then top with a quail egg, pointy-end up.

Grind the celery seeds and sea salt in a mortar and pestle or coffee grinder. Sprinkle the celery salt over each egg and top with lumpfish roe, if using, and nigella seeds.

Makes 20

20 quail eggs (available from good butchers
   and poultry suppliers)
½ cup good-quality mayonnaise
20 mini vol au vent cases
1 handful curly endive
2 teaspoons celery seeds
2 teaspoons sea salt
lumpfish roe (optional)
2 tablespoons nigella seeds (available from
   food halls and spice shops)

Spicy lamb and pine nut fingers with pomegranate sauce

I love these little lamb pastries – they are a little fiddly to make but you will be rewarded with a fantastic finished product. You can freeze the uncooked fingers, then bake them just before you're ready to serve. Recipe pictured following pages.

Heat the olive oil in a large frying pan over medium heat. Add the lamb and cook until browned, using the back of a wooden spoon to break up the pieces. Add the shallots and garlic and cook for 3–4 minutes. Add the sumac, cumin, baharat, coriander, pine nuts and currants, stir well and remove from the heat. Cool slightly, then add the haloumi and lemon juice to taste. Check the seasoning.

Preheat the oven to 220°C and line two or three baking trays with baking paper. Place one sheet of pastry on a work surface and cut it lengthways into three equal strips. Brush the long edges of each strip with butter. Place 1 tablespoon of the lamb mixture at the end of each strip, fold the edges in and roll into a large cigar shape. Repeat with the remaining pastry sheets and filling. (Cover the pastry with a damp tea towel as you go so it doesn't dry out.)

Brush melted butter on the top of the rolls, place on the baking trays and bake for 10–15 minutes or until golden and cooked.

To make the pomegranate sauce, combine the ingredients in a bowl.

Dress a serving platter with coriander leaves and pomegranate seeds. Place the lamb fingers on top and drizzle with the sauce.

Makes 30–40

2 tablespoons olive oil
350 g lamb mince
6 golden shallots, chopped
3 cloves garlic, finely chopped
1 tablespoon sumac (see glossary)
1 tablespoon ground cumin
1 tablespoon baharat (see glossary)
1 handful coriander leaves, chopped,
   plus extra leaves to garnish
50 g pine nuts
½ cup currants, brought to the boil in enough
   red wine vinegar to cover, then drained
100 g haloumi cheese, crumbled
½ lemon, juiced
sea salt and freshly ground black pepper
185 g filo pastry
melted butter, for brushing
1 pomegranate, seeded, to garnish

Pomegranate sauce
100 ml pomegranate molasses (see glossary)
2 tablespoons olive oil
1 tablespoon lemon juice

Spicy lamb and pine nut fingers
with pomegranate sauce (see page 25)

Sourdough open sandwiches with crab, avocado, chervil and mayonnaise

I'm sure I don't have to talk you into making these: crab and avocado – what's not to like? Cooked blue swimmer crabmeat is available from fish markets and fish shops (though you may need to order it in advance).

Lightly toast the bread slices.

Combine the mayonnaise, yoghurt, salt, pepper and a little lemon juice in a bowl. Add the crabmeat and green onion and mix well.

Spread the mixture over the toast and top with avocado slices. Sprinkle with chervil and drizzle with olive oil. Scatter the fried shallots over the top, add more lemon juice if desired, then sprinkle with salt and serve.

Makes 6

1 large loaf sourdough bread, cut into 6 slices
   approximately 6 cm × 14 cm
100 ml good-quality mayonnaise
75 g plain yoghurt
sea salt and freshly ground black pepper
1 lemon, juiced
250 g cooked blue swimmer crabmeat
½ bunch green onions, finely sliced
2 ripe avocados, sliced
handful of chervil sprigs
3 tablespoons extra virgin olive oil
¼ cup fried shallots (available from Asian food stores)

Roasted eggplant strips with oregano and chilli

These eggplant strips have a smooth, velvety texture. Dress the eggplant while it's still warm so it will absorb the delicious flavours. Best served on the day as part of a grazing selection, with grilled lamb cutlets and lemon, or simply eaten with fresh bread.

Preheat the oven to 180°C. Line a baking tray with baking paper.

Cut the eggplants lengthways into 2 cm thick slices. Brush the eggplant slices with 100 ml olive oil, then place in a single layer on the baking tray. Bake for about 15 minutes or until soft.

Meanwhile, combine the chillies, salt and garlic in a large mortar and pestle and pound until combined. Add the oregano and pound for 2–4 minutes until you have a rough green paste, then stir in the vinegar and remaining olive oil.

Cut the cooked eggplant into strips, pour on the dressing and stir to combine. Serve immediately or store in the fridge for up to 2 days.

Serves 10–12 as an antipasto

4 large eggplants (aubergines)
250 ml olive oil
3 small red chillies
1–2 tablespoons sea salt
3 cloves garlic
½ bunch oregano, leaves chopped
100 ml red wine vinegar

Cannellini beans with rosemary, prawns and lemon

Be generous with this cannellini paste. The velvety texture is superb on toast, and the fried prawns, garlic and rosemary make a beautifully rustic combination.

Heat 3 tablespoons olive oil in a medium frying pan over medium heat. Add the sliced garlic and cook for 3 minutes, then season with salt. Add the cannellini beans, stock or water and rosemary and cook for about 8 minutes or until the beans are very soft. Remove from the heat and drain (reserve the liquid).

Mash the beans with a fork or the back of a spoon (add some of the reserved liquid if the paste is too dry) and drizzle with 3 tablespoons olive oil and a squeeze of lemon.

Toast the bread and rub generously with the whole garlic clove. Spread with the mashed cannellini beans.

Heat 4 tablespoons olive oil in a frying pan over medium heat. When hot, add the chopped prawns and cook until they just change colour. Season, then add the parsley and a squeeze of lemon. Spoon the prawns over the beans and season with a generous grinding of black pepper.

Serves 8 as a starter or antipasto

200 ml extra virgin olive oil
2 cloves garlic, sliced, plus 1 extra clove, peeled
 and left whole
sea salt and freshly ground black pepper
2 × 400 g cans cannellini beans, drained
500–600 ml stock or water
3 sprigs rosemary, leaves chopped and ground in
 a mortar and pestle with a little sea salt.
1 lemon
8 thin slices baguette or 4 large slices rustic bread,
 cut in half
5 large green (raw) prawns, peeled, deveined
 and chopped
1 handful flat-leaf parsley leaves, torn

Bacalao-style trevally with sautéed endive

You can make a luscious fish paste from the salted cod you see hanging in continental delis. I like to make my own version – allow 12 hours to salt the fish, and don't skimp on the garlic. Full of flavour, it's the perfect start to a meal.

Serves 8–10

4 cups rock salt

500 g trevally or blue-eye (choose a thick fillet), skin and bones removed

1 litre milk

1 bay leaf

8 whole peppercorns

3 cloves garlic, sliced

2 large desiree potatoes, boiled and pushed through a mouli (food mill), fine sieve or ricer

sea salt and freshly ground black pepper

2 lemons, juiced

125 ml extra virgin olive oil

8 slices sourdough bread, drizzled with olive oil and toasted, then halved

125 ml vinaigrette (shop-bought or made with equal parts olive oil and white wine vinegar and seasoned to taste)

3 handfuls curly endive

1 handful pitted olives (optional)

lemon halves, to serve

Place half the salt in a plastic or ceramic container and sit the fish on top. Cover with the remaining salt, then cover and place in the fridge for 12 hours. Remove the fish and rinse thoroughly under cold running water.

Bring the milk to the boil in a large saucepan over medium heat. Add the bay leaf, peppercorns, 2 cloves garlic and the fish and simmer for 6–8 minutes. Remove the fish (check that it's cooked) and transfer to a food processor. Add the potatoes, salt, remaining garlic and half the lemon juice and process. Drizzle in the oil until the mixture is smooth and creamy. Add some black pepper and the remaining lemon juice. Spread the fish mixture thickly on the bread.

Place the vinaigrette in a medium frying pan over medium heat. Add the endive and allow to wilt. Add the olives, if using, and cook, stirring, for 2 minutes. Spoon the endive mixture over the fish and serve with lemon halves on the side.

Shaved fennel, orange, red onion and black olive salad

Serve this zesty salad with grilled lamb cutlets or Moorish pork skewers (see page 184). It also works well with grilled or baked fish – simply add lemon and lime segments and a few handfuls of your favourite salad greens.

Combine the fennel, orange segments, onion, olives and gherkins in a large bowl.

Place the orange zest and juice, olive oil, salt and pepper in a small bowl and whisk until combined. Pour the dressing over the salad and set aside for 15 minutes. Serve scattered with parsley.

Serves 4

1 large bulb fennel, trimmed and very finely sliced

1 orange, zested, cut into segments and juice reserved

2 large blood oranges, zested, cut into segments and juice reserved

1 small red onion, finely sliced

¾ cup black olives

4 small gherkins, finely chopped

100 ml olive oil

sea salt and freshly ground black pepper

6 sprigs flat-leaf parsley, chopped

> Prosciutto with figs and fresh goat's curd

The fresh, sharp flavour of goat's curd is the perfect complement to the saltiness of prosciutto and the sweetness of figs. For a formal dinner, serve this salad on individual plates as a starter. For a more casual affair, let your guests help themselves from a big platter in the middle of the table.

Arrange half the prosciutto over a large platter. Scatter with the rocket and mint, then place the remaining prosciutto over the rocket. Top with the fig slices and dollops of goat's curd. Season well with salt and pepper.

Whisk the sherry vinegar and olive oil in a small bowl until combined. Drizzle the dressing over the salad and serve with grissini or crusty bread.

Serves 4–6

12 thin slices prosciutto

6 handfuls rocket leaves

6 sprigs mint, leaves torn and washed

6 ripe green or black figs, stems removed and thickly sliced

100 g fresh goat's curd (see glossary)

sea salt and freshly ground black pepper

3 tablespoons sherry vinegar

125 ml extra virgin olive oil

grissini or crusty bread, to serve

Butter lettuce with cherry tomatoes and mozzarella

This is the ultimate barbecue salad. It goes with just about everything and you can throw it together at the last minute. You can use light sour cream or yoghurt instead of the pouring cream but don't leave it out altogether – it makes the salad taste so much better.

Combine half the olive oil and half the vinegar in a bowl with the capers, cream and mozzarella or bocconcini. Set aside.

In a separate bowl, combine the tomatoes, onion, basil and parsley, then toss with the remaining oil and vinegar.

Spread the lettuce on a serving platter and top with the mozzarella and tomato mixtures. Serve immediately.

Serves 4

100 ml extra virgin olive oil
1½ tablespoons red wine vinegar
2 tablespoons capers, coarsely chopped
100 ml pouring cream
1 buffalo mozzarella or 100 g bocconcini, torn or cut into chunks
½ punnet cherry tomatoes, halved
½ red onion, finely sliced
2 sprigs basil, leaves only, torn
2 sprigs flat-leaf parsley, leaves only, torn
1 large butter lettuce, cut into quarters

> Shredded cabbage, mushroom and herb salad

This salad is great on its own, but also goes perfectly with any spicy Asian-style chicken or pork dish – try it with braised honey, soy and ginger spare ribs (see page 174). For non-meat eaters, serve it with pressed, seasoned tofu or grilled or pan-fried fish.

Combine the olive oil, soy sauce, salt and green chilli in a bowl. Add the mushrooms and stir to combine. Set aside for 5 minutes.

Place the remaining ingredients in a large bowl and toss to combine. Stir in the mushroom mixture and serve immediately.

Serves 6

100 ml extra virgin olive oil
2½ tablespoons light soy sauce
sea salt, to taste
1 green chilli, finely sliced
10 Swiss brown mushrooms, finely sliced
½ small cabbage, finely shredded
3 cm piece fresh ginger, cut into very fine matchsticks
½ bunch Thai basil, leaves only
2 sprigs dill, leaves only
5 sprigs mint, leaves only
8 cm piece white radish (daikon), peeled and cut into very fine matchsticks
1 clove garlic, finely chopped
½ lime, juiced

< Rainbow chard, fetta and dukkah eggs

This reminds me of the delicious omelettes my mum used to make. My additions are fetta and dukkah, an Egyptian blend of toasted nuts and spices that I keep in a sealed container in the fridge.

Heat the olive oil in a large, deep frying pan over medium heat and cook the onion and garlic for 2 minutes. Add the chard or silverbeet, season and stir. Cook over high heat for 2 minutes, then add the water and simmer, covered, for 10 minutes or until tender.

Crack the eggs into the pan and crumble the fetta over the top. Sprinkle with three-quarters of the dukkah and cook, covered, over medium heat for 2–3 minutes or until the eggs are cooked to your liking. Pour on the lemon juice. Remove from the heat, sprinkle with the remaining dukkah and serve with toast and lemon wedges, if using.

Serves 2

4 tablespoons olive oil
½ red onion, halved and sliced
1 clove garlic, finely sliced
1 bunch rainbow chard or silverbeet, stems trimmed
    and chopped into 1 cm pieces
sea salt and freshly ground black pepper
200 ml water
3 free-range eggs
100 g fetta
2 tablespoons dukkah (see glossary)
½ lemon, juiced
toasted bread fingers, to serve
lemon wedges, to serve (optional)

Porcini and potato bake with thyme

Kipfler potatoes are now readily available from most supermarkets and greengrocers. This hearty potato dish is the perfect accompaniment to roast beef or chicken.

Preheat the oven to 220°C. Lightly grease a shallow baking dish.

Cook the potatoes in a saucepan of boiling water for 5 minutes, then drain. Soak the porcini mushrooms in ½ cup boiling water for about 10 minutes, then drain and chop.

Place the potatoes in the baking dish in a single layer and add the mushrooms, thyme and olive oil. Season with salt and pepper, then drizzle the cream over the potatoes. Pour on the stock and sprinkle with parmesan. Cover with foil and bake for 30 minutes. Remove the foil and bake for a further 10 minutes or until golden.

Serves 4–6

8 large kipfler potatoes, unpeeled,
    sliced lengthways
10 g dried porcini mushrooms
5 sprigs thyme, leaves only
100 ml extra virgin olive oil
sea salt and freshly ground black pepper
100 ml thickened cream
150 ml chicken stock (see page 134)
50 g grated parmesan

Caponata

Caponata is such a versatile dish. Serve it warm or at room temperature as part of an antipasto platter or as an accompaniment to crumbed meat, fish or chicken. Try tossing it through pasta or serve it with couscous and a generous dollop of plain yoghurt.

Preheat the oven to 220°C. Brush the capsicums with a little olive oil, place in an ovenproof dish and bake for about 20 minutes or until the skin is blistered. Transfer to a medium bowl, cover with plastic film and set aside for 25–30 minutes. Peel, seed and cut into strips.

Reduce the oven temperature to 200°C. Combine the eggplant, onion, garlic and oregano in a large baking dish, season well, and drizzle with the remaining olive oil. Cover tightly with a lid or foil and bake for 20–30 minutes. Stir then bake, covered, for a further 15 minutes or until the onion is very soft.

Add a squeeze of lemon and the remaining ingredients, including the capsicum. Stir well, then cover and bake for 30–40 minutes or until the eggplant is soft. Allow to cool slightly, then squeeze lemon juice over the top, to taste.

Serves 6–8 as a starter or antipasto

2 large red capsicums (peppers)
185 ml extra virgin olive oil
2 large eggplants (aubergines), cut into 1–2 cm pieces
2 red onions, sliced
4 cloves garlic, finely sliced
½ bunch oregano, leaves only
sea salt and freshly ground black pepper
1 lemon
12–14 cherry tomatoes on the vine, snipped into
   little branches of 2 or 3 tomatoes
2 handfuls flat-leaf parsley leaves
2 tablespoons capers
handful pitted green olives
handful pitted black olives
2 tablespoons castor sugar
100 ml red wine vinegar
200 g crushed tomatoes
100 ml dry white wine

Peach and witlof salad with mustard dressing

Sweet, fragrant peaches say summer to me. This salad is perfect with grilled pork sausages or chops, or try it with braised organic bacon (see page 174).

Combine the witlof leaves, watercress and peaches in a large bowl.

Mix together the vinaigrette and mustards in a small bowl, season to taste and stir until smooth. Add the dressing to the salad and toss gently to combine. Serve immediately.

Serves 4–6

4 witlof (Belgian endive), leaves separated and trimmed
1 bunch watercress
2 ripe peaches, sliced into rounds
125 ml vinaigrette dressing (store-bought or made with 3 parts olive oil and 1 part white wine vinegar and seasoned to taste)
3 teaspoons seeded mustard
1 teaspoon Dijon mustard
sea salt and freshly ground black pepper

> Tuna salad with flat bread, paprika and baharat

Adding fried bread gives another dimension to everyday tuna salad, and exotic spices bring the humblest of ingredients to life. This is one of my new favourite recipes, inspired by the cooking tales of Melbourne chef Greg Malouf in his beautiful book, Saha.

Toss the bread with the baharat and olive oil in a large frying pan over high heat for about 2 minutes or until the bread is crisp. Add a little salt and remove from the heat.

Mix the remaining ingredients (except the lemon juice) in a large bowl. Top with the bread, drizzle with the lemon juice and serve immediately with lemon wedges, if using.

Serves 4

2 round flat breads, rolled up and thinly sliced into long strips
1 teaspoon baharat (see glossary)
160 ml extra virgin olive oil
sea salt
2 × 185 g cans tuna in chilli oil
2 small Lebanese cucumbers, cut into quarters lengthways
2 large tomatoes, chopped
1 red onion, sliced
dash of Tabasco sauce
1 teaspoon sweet paprika
splash of sherry vinegar
2 handfuls torn basil or flat-leaf parsley leaves
1 lemon, juiced
lemon wedges, to serve (optional)

Summer minestrone

The green vegetables really sing in this fresh summer soup, and the traditional dollop of pesto is just delicious. It is best eaten on the day it is made as the vegetables discolour quickly.

To make the pesto, put the basil, parsley, pine nuts, parmesan and garlic in a food processor and process to a fine paste. Add the oil and scrape down the bowl. Process until smooth, then season to taste.

For the minestrone, heat the oil and butter in a large, wide-based saucepan over medium–low heat. Add the onion, garlic, carrot and celery and cook for 8–10 minutes until sticky and slightly caramelised. Season with salt.

Add the remaining vegetables and the mixed herbs and increase the heat to high. Sauté for a few minutes, then add the stock and cannellini beans. Stir well and bring to the boil for 2 minutes, then remove from the heat and season to taste.

To serve, ladle into warmed bowls and top with a spoonful of pesto and a good drizzle of extra virgin olive oil.

Serves 6–8

100 ml extra virgin olive oil
50 g butter
1 onion, finely diced
6 cloves garlic, sliced
½ bunch Dutch (baby) carrots, finely sliced
1 celery heart, sliced
sea salt and freshly ground black pepper
2 zucchini (courgettes), sliced
¾ cup fresh peas
1 bunch asparagus, sliced into short lengths
12 green beans, cut into short lengths
1 cup mixed chopped herbs (such as parsley, basil and oregano)
1.25 litres chicken stock
400 g can cannellini beans, drained
extra virgin olive oil, for drizzling

Basil pesto

2 big bunches basil, leaves only
½ bunch flat-leaf parsley, leaves only
100 g pine nuts
120 g parmesan, grated
2 cloves garlic, chopped
150–200 ml olive oil
sea salt and freshly ground black pepper

Iceberg lettuce, watercress and avocado salad

This is a fantastic salad to pair with grilled steak or barbecued fish. Finely shaved fennel would be a beautiful addition too.

Arrange the lettuce in a large bowl, and top with the avocado, watercress and parsley.

Whisk the olive oil, lemon juice, mustard, salt and pepper in a small bowl until smooth. Pour the dressing over the salad, toss and serve immediately.

Serves 4

1 small iceberg lettuce, core removed
  and finely sliced
1 ripe avocado, chopped
½ bunch watercress
2 handfuls flat-leaf parsley, torn
125 ml extra virgin olive oil
1 lemon, juiced
2 teaspoons Dijon mustard
sea salt and freshly ground black pepper

Braised witlof with ham and gruyère

I like to serve this Flemish-inspired dish as a light lunch or starter or as an accompaniment to roast pork or beef. The bitter witlof complements the ham and the rich nuttiness of the gruyère. Recipe pictured following pages.

Preheat the oven to 200°C. Trim the base of the witlof and hollow out the cores, leaving the witlof whole.

Melt the butter in a large frying pan over medium heat. Add the witlof, season with salt and pepper and cook, turning, until brown. Add the ginger and garlic and cook for 3–4 minutes. Stir in the stock and simmer for 10 minutes or until the witlof is cooked but still firm.

Remove the witlof from the pan, add the cream and cook over high heat for 2 minutes.

Place the witlof in a baking dish and sprinkle with ham. Pour the cream mixture over the top, and sprinkle with the thyme and gruyère. Bake for 20–25 minutes or until golden. Serve with a dressed bitter-leaf salad.

Serves 4

8 witlof (Belgian endive)
40 g unsalted butter
sea salt and freshly ground black pepper
3 cm piece fresh ginger, finely grated
1 clove garlic, finely chopped
600 ml chicken or veal stock
125 ml pouring cream
150 g leg ham, roughly chopped into batons
2 sprigs thyme, leaves only
150 g grated gruyère cheese

Braised witlof with ham
and gruyère (see page 49)

Roasted Dutch carrots with honey and thyme

Roasting carrots enhances their natural sweetness and leaving the skin on ensures all the goodness is locked in. For a side dish that is superb with roast beef, parsnips and turnips can be added: simply substitute half the carrots with 1 turnip and 2 parsnips, peeled and cut into quarters.

Preheat the oven to 190°C. Place the carrots in a baking dish and toss with the olive oil. Sprinkle the thyme over the top and bake for 35 minutes, turning occasionally.

Remove from the oven, add the honey and butter and toss to coat. Bake for 3 minutes more or until the carrots are cooked.

Serves 6

2 bunches Dutch (baby) carrots, scrubbed
  and trimmed
1 tablespoon olive oil
4 large sprigs thyme, leaves only
3 tablespoons honey
60 g unsalted butter

> Roasted pumpkin with cinnamon, pine nuts and yoghurt

I like the smooth texture and deep golden colour of jap pumpkin, especially with the skin on as it adds a lovely, chewy contrast. Serve this versatile dish as a starter, as an accompaniment to roast chicken or lamb, or as a main meal with rice and salad.

Preheat the oven to 200°C. Place the pumpkin, olive oil and cinnamon in a bowl, season with salt and pepper and toss to combine. Transfer to a baking tray and bake for about 30–40 minutes or until golden and cooked.

Arrange the pumpkin on a serving platter and drizzle with the yoghurt. Pour on the lemon juice and scatter the pine nuts, chilli and coriander leaves over the top. Best served at room temperature when all the flavours have melded together.

Serves 4 as a starter or side dish

½ jap pumpkin, unpeeled, seeded
  and cut into 8 slices
100 ml olive oil
2 teaspoons ground cinnamon
sea salt and freshly ground black pepper
1 cup plain yoghurt
½ lemon, juiced
4 tablespoons pine nuts, toasted
1 small red chilli, very finely sliced
6 sprigs coriander, leaves only

< Spinach, rice and yoghurt salad with almonds

Rice goes beautifully with yoghurt. This healthy, addictive salad is a great palate soother if you're having spicy food, and is delicious with fish or lamb cutlets.

Place the cooked rice in a large bowl. Add the spinach, parsley, peas, almonds and onion and stir well.

Combine the yoghurt, lemon juice and olive oil in a small bowl. Season to taste, stir until smooth, then pour over the rice mixture. Top with crushed toasted almonds.

Serves 6

3 cups cooked long-grain rice, kept warm
4 handfuls English spinach, shredded
1 bunch flat-leaf parsley, finely chopped
1 cup cooked peas
¼ cup toasted almonds
½ large red onion, sliced
1½ cups plain yoghurt
1 lemon, juiced
100 ml extra virgin olive oil
sea salt and freshly ground black pepper
toasted almonds, extra, crushed

Whipped potato baked with taleggio

Serve this rich, creamy side dish with roast lamb, beef or as part of a vegetarian feast.

Preheat the oven to 200°C.

Cook the potatoes in lightly salted boiling water for 10–15 minutes until tender. Drain and press through a mouli (food mill), fine sieve or ricer.

Combine the cream and butter in a saucepan over medium heat and bring to a simmer. Remove from the heat and stir into the mashed potato with a wooden spoon.

Fold in most of the parmesan, reserving enough to sprinkle on top. Season well with salt and pepper. Fold in the taleggio and spoon the mixture into a baking dish. Top with the remaining parmesan and bake for 20 minutes or until golden.

Serves 6

1 kg desiree potatoes, chopped
400 ml pouring cream
100 g unsalted butter, chopped
80 g grated parmesan
sea salt and freshly ground black pepper
120 g taleggio cheese (see glossary), chopped

Potato, porcini and barley soup

Rustic, filling and delicious, a big bowl of this thick soup eaten on the lounge makes a classy TV dinner.

Place the barley in a small saucepan and cover with water. Bring to the boil over medium heat, then simmer for 25–30 minutes or until tender. Drain.

Meanwhile, place the porcini mushrooms in a small saucepan and cover with water. Bring to the boil, then simmer for 3 minutes. Drain and chop, reserving the cooking liquid.

Heat the butter and olive oil in a large saucepan over medium heat, add the onion, garlic and leek and cook for 5 minutes or until soft. Add the thyme, porcini and field mushrooms and cook for 8–10 minutes. Stir in the potatoes, then add the porcini liquid, chicken stock and 4 cups water and simmer for about 10 minutes or until the potatoes are cooked. Add the cream and simmer for 5–8 minutes.

Transfer the soup to a food processor or blender and process until smooth. Return to the saucepan, add the barley and bring to a simmer. Serve with a drizzle of olive oil and toasted rye bread on the side.

Serves 8

½ cup barley
35 g dried porcini mushrooms
40 g unsalted butter
4 tablespoons olive oil, plus extra to serve
2 onions, sliced
4 cloves garlic, chopped
1 leek, trimmed and sliced
3 sprigs thyme, leaves only
6–8 field mushrooms, stems and caps chopped
4 potatoes, finely sliced
500 ml chicken stock (see page 134)
250 ml pouring cream
finely sliced rye bread, toasted until crisp, to serve

Sauteed zucchini with herbs
and lemon (see page 60)

Sauteed zucchini with herbs and lemon

This dish is a great alternative to the less exciting option of steaming or boiling zucchini, and works well as an accompaniment to grilled meat or fish, or as part of an antipasto starter. If you can, use white zucchini – they're a beautiful pale green and have a lovely subtle flavour. Recipe pictured previous pages.

Slice the zucchini lengthways into 5 mm thick strips. Heat a large non-stick frying pan over medium heat and add half the oil. Place half the zucchini in a single layer in the pan and cook over high heat for 2–3 minutes or until golden. Season with salt and pepper, then turn and cook the other side. Remove from the pan and cook the rest of the zucchini in the remaining olive oil.

Return all the zucchini to the pan, squeeze the lemon juice over the top and sprinkle with the herbs. Serve warm.

Serves 4

5 white or green zucchini (courgettes)
100 ml olive oil
sea salt and freshly ground black pepper
1 lemon, juiced
4 sprigs flat-leaf parsley, leaves only
4 sprigs oregano, leaves only

> Winter tabbouleh

This unusual but really yummy salad is a little heavier than traditional tabbouleh and the flavours are more intense, with a sweet and sour cinnamon dressing. Serve it with grilled quail, chicken, roast lamb or fish.

Preheat the oven to 175°C. Roast the cauliflower on a lightly greased baking tray for 25 minutes. Set aside to cool.

To make the dressing, combine the ingredients in a small bowl. Stir well and set aside for about 5 minutes.

Combine the cauliflower, burghul, fennel, onion, almonds, parsley and pomegranate seeds, if using, in a large bowl. Add the dressing and toss gently.

Serves 6–8

1 cauliflower, broken into florets and stems sliced
¾ cup fine burghul (see glossary), soaked in 250 ml boiling water for 10 minutes, then squeezed dry
½ bulb fennel, trimmed and finely sliced
1 red onion, finely sliced
½ cup blanched almonds, lightly toasted
8 sprigs flat-leaf parsley, chopped
½ cup pomegranate seeds (optional; see glossary)

Dressing

3 tablespoons pomegranate molasses (see glossary)
½ teaspoon sea salt
1 teaspoon ground cinnamon
1 lemon, juiced
2 teaspoons sugar
100 ml extra virgin olive oil
½ clove garlic, very finely chopped
freshly ground black pepper

Brown rice, mint and pine nut salad with currants and caramelised onion

This salad is delicious on its own or with grilled haloumi. Brown rice is often overlooked for salads but it has a lovely nutty flavour that is enhanced when paired with pine nuts and currants.

Heat 4 tablespoons olive oil in a large non-stick frying pan over low heat. Add the onion, season well with salt and pepper and cook, stirring occasionally, for about 20–30 minutes or until the onion is caramelised. Stir in the currants and vinegar.

Combine the cooked rice, parsley, mint and chilli in a large bowl. Stir in the lemon juice and remaining olive oil, then add half the onions and half the pine nuts and toss to combine. Top with the remaining onions and pine nuts.

Serves 6

125 ml olive oil

3 brown onions, halved and sliced

sea salt and freshly ground black pepper

150 g currants, just covered with red wine vinegar and boiled for 3 minutes until the liquid has almost evaporated (reserve liquid)

2 cups cooked brown rice, kept warm

½ bunch flat-leaf parsley, leaves only

½ bunch mint, leaves only

2 green chillies, finely sliced

2 lemons, juiced

120 g pine nuts, toasted

White cabbage, radish, mint and caraway salad

Delicious with fried fish, veal schnitzel, sausages or roast pork, this cabbage dish will also liven up a sandwich the next day and give traditional coleslaw a nudge.

Combine the cabbage, mint, radish and onion in a large bowl.

Place the caraway seeds, lemon juice, olive oil, salt and pepper in a small bowl and whisk until smooth. Pour the dressing over the cabbage mixture and toss gently to combine. Set aside for 5 minutes before serving.

Serves 6

½ cabbage, very finely shredded

6 sprigs mint, leaves torn

6 red radishes, very finely sliced

½ red onion, finely chopped

1½ teaspoons ground caraway seeds

½ lemon, juiced

100 ml extra virgin olive oil

sea salt and freshly ground black pepper

Carrot and oregano salad with lentils and red wine vinegar

The roasted garlic dressing is as luscious as mayonnaise and gives this salad a buttery, nutty flavour. Serve it as part of an antipasto platter, with pasta or with grilled lamb or chicken.

Slice the carrots into thin ribbons (you can use a mandolin or vegetable peeler to do this). Bring a medium saucepan of water to the boil, add the carrots and blanch for 15 seconds. Drain.

Combine the vinegar and olive oil in a medium bowl. Squeeze the roasted garlic cloves out of their skins and add to the bowl, then whisk in the oregano, salt and pepper. Add the onion and stir to combine. Stir in the carrots and lentils, while still warm, and the parsley. Set aside for 10 minutes before serving.

Serves 4

1 bunch Dutch (baby) carrots, trimmed and peeled
100 ml red wine vinegar
100 ml extra virgin olive oil
2 large bulbs garlic, brushed with olive oil and roasted at 150°C for 30 minutes
6 sprigs oregano, leaves finely chopped
sea salt and freshly ground black pepper
½ red onion, finely chopped
½ cup small green red lentils, simmered in boiling water for 15 minutes, then drained
½ bunch flat-leaf parsley, leaves only

Hard-boiled egg curry with spinach, tomato, ginger and yoghurt

When I first made this curry, I had a few bits and pieces in the fridge and an almost-bare cupboard. It turned out to be a success and can be a surprisingly filling meal when eaten with steamed rice. I've also served it with roast chicken rubbed with a garlic, pepper and chilli spice mix. Recipe pictured following pages.

Heat the olive oil in a heavy-based saucepan over medium heat. Add the onion, garlic and ginger and cook for 4 minutes. Stir in the mustard seeds and a large pinch of salt, then add the chilli, remaining spices and sugar and cook for 1 minute. Add the tomatoes and stock or water, then simmer over low heat for 8–10 minutes.

Add the spinach and yoghurt and cook for a further 8–10 minutes. Add the eggs and check the seasoning. Stir in the coriander leaves and serve with steamed rice.

Serves 4–6

100 ml olive oil
3 large brown onions, halved and sliced
5 cloves garlic, chopped
80 g fresh ginger, cut into matchsticks
2 tablespoons mustard seeds
sea salt and freshly ground black pepper
2 large red chillies, cut in half lengthways
3 teaspoons ground turmeric
3 teaspoons ground coriander
2 teaspoons ground cumin
½ teaspoon Chinese five-spice powder
3 tablespoons castor sugar
400 g can chopped tomatoes
250 ml chicken stock (see page 134) or water
4 large handfuls baby spinach, shredded
1 cup plain yoghurt
8 hard-boiled free-range eggs, peeled and halved
1 bunch coriander, leaves only

Hard-boiled egg curry with spinach,
tomato, ginger and yoghurt (see page 63)

Asparagus with poached egg and prosciutto

This combination is terrific for brunch or lunch. If you're feeling decadent, use white asparagus and drizzle it with a little truffle oil and freshly shaved truffle.

Bring a saucepan of salted water to the boil over medium heat. Add the asparagus and cook for 3–4 minutes, then drain. Toss with the butter and season with salt and pepper.

Bring a large saucepan of water to the boil over high heat, pour in the vinegar and reduce the heat to low. Carefully add the eggs and poach for 3–4 minutes. Use a slotted spoon to remove the eggs, then drain and keep warm.

To serve, divide the asparagus among four shallow bowls and top each with an egg and some prosciutto. Scatter with chives and chervil and sprinkle with parmesan. Season with salt and pepper and serve with toast, if using.

Serves 4

2 bunches asparagus, peeled
150 g unsalted butter, chopped
sea salt and freshly ground black pepper
1 tablespoon vinegar
4 free-range eggs
8 slices prosciutto
2 tablespoons finely chopped chives
5 sprigs chervil, coarsely chopped
150 g shaved parmesan
buttered toast, to serve (optional)

Bresaola and cabbage salad

This fresh and tasty salad is so popular it's one of our specials at the Melbourne Wine Room for more than half the year.

To make the dressing, combine the lemon juice and olive oil in a small bowl, season with salt and pepper and whisk well.

In a large bowl, combine the cabbage, fennel and parsley, season and toss with a splash of the dressing.

Place the bresaola on a platter and scatter with the cabbage mixture. Top with the parmesan, remaining dressing and freshly ground pepper.

Serves 6 as a starter

½ lemon, juiced
100 ml extra virgin olive oil
sea salt and freshly ground black pepper
3 cups finely shredded cabbage
½ bulb fennel, finely sliced
5 sprigs flat-leaf parsley, leaves only
18 slices bresaola
100 g shaved parmesan

Grape, burghul and witlof salad

This ambrosian salad is a refreshing accompaniment for roasted meats. Try it with black pepper, walnut and cumin-stuffed chicken roasted with pumpkin (see page 158).

Combine the oil and verjuice in a bowl, season well and stir in the parsley, mint and onion. Toss in the burghul, witlof and grapes and serve.

Serves 4–6

4 tablespoons extra virgin olive oil

3 tablespoons verjuice (see glossary)

sea salt and freshly ground black pepper

2 handfuls flat-leaf parsley, leaves torn

2 handfuls mint, leaves torn

½ red onion, finely diced

100 g coarse burghul (see glossary),
    soaked in 125 ml boiling water for 10 minutes,
    then squeezed dry

2 witlof (Belgian endive), trimmed and leaves
    separated

1 bunch red or green grapes, sliced

Cauliflower, fennel and leek in white sauce with provolone

There's something so comforting about cauliflower and cheese sauce. Try this luxurious version with the added flavours of fennel and provolone, an Italian semi-hard cow's milk cheese. Recipe pictured following pages.

Bring a large saucepan of lightly salted water to the boil (leave enough room for all the vegetables), add the fennel and cook, covered, over medium heat for 10 minutes. Add the whole cauliflower and cook for 8 minutes. Add the leeks and cook for a further 5 minutes or until all the vegetables are just tender. Drain and set aside.

Preheat the oven to 190°C. Lightly grease a large ovenproof dish.

For the sauce, combine the milk and bay leaf in a pan and bring to a simmer. Remove from the heat.

Melt the butter in a medium saucepan over medium heat. Add the flour and stir until smooth. Gradually add the milk, stirring constantly, and cook for 6 minutes or until the mixture coats the back of a wooden spoon. Season with salt and pepper, remove the bay leaf and stir in half the cheese. Set aside.

Slice the fennel lengthways and arrange in the ovenproof dish. Cut the cauliflower into thick slices and place on top of the fennel. Scatter the leek over the top. Pour the white sauce over the vegetables and sprinkle with the remaining cheese. Bake for 25–30 minutes or until the top is golden.

Serves 6–8

1 large bulb fennel, trimmed

1 small cauliflower, trimmed

4 leeks, washed, trimmed and cut into 4 cm slices

650 ml milk

1 bay leaf

30 g unsalted butter, chopped

30 g plain (all-purpose) flour

sea salt and freshly ground black pepper

120 g provolone, grated

Cauliflower, fennel and leek in
white sauce with provolone (see page 67)

Tunisian pumpkin salad

I grew up eating this North African-influenced salad and it's still a regular feature on my menus. It goes exceptionally well with fish, and tastes just as great the next day.

Preheat the oven to 240°C and lightly grease a baking tray.

Heat the oil in a large saucepan over high heat. When very hot, add the capsicums and deep-fry for 3–5 minutes or until starting to brown. Transfer to a bowl, cover and allow to rest.

Toss the pumpkin with the olive oil and cumin, season with salt and pepper and place on the baking tray. Bake for 25 minutes or until soft and cooked. Cool slightly, then chop coarsely.

Peel the capsicums and chop coarsely. Place the capsicum and pumpkin in a bowl and add lemon juice to taste and season generously. Serve at room temperature.

Serves 4–6

oil, for deep-frying
1 red capsicum (pepper), seeded and cut into quarters
4 green capsicums (peppers), seeded and cut into quarters
½ jap pumpkin, seeded and cut into 3 cm cubes
100 ml olive oil
2 tablespoons ground cumin
2–3 tablespoons sea salt, or to taste
freshly ground black pepper
1 tablespoon lemon juice

> Braised peas with cos lettuce and mint

This classic French side dish is usually made with iceberg lettuce but I've used cos because I prefer its coarser texture, and I really like to make the lettuce a feature. Serve it with roast chicken or lamb, or pan-seared fish. Peas and lettuce never tasted so good.

Melt half the butter in a very large frying pan over medium heat and cook the garlic for 2 minutes. Add the peas, lettuce and ¼ cup water, stir and simmer for about 5 minutes.

Add the mint, salt, sugar and remaining butter and simmer for 3 minutes or until the vegetables are tender and the sauce is glossy and syrupy.

Serves 4–6

80 g unsalted butter
1 large clove garlic, sliced
2½ cups frozen peas
2 cos lettuces, trimmed and cut into 1 cm slices
5 sprigs mint, leaves torn
1 level tablespoon sea salt, or to taste
2 tablespoons castor sugar

Figs with gorgonzola, toasted walnuts and honey

Figs come in and out of season in a flash so when they're at their peak, I find ways to use them for breakfast, lunch and dinner. This dish makes a wonderful starter, or serve it at the end of a meal in place of cheese or dessert.

Drizzle the lemon juice over the fig slices and set aside.

Place the mascarpone in a medium bowl, add 2 tablespoons water and mix until smooth. Stir in the gorgonzola, adding a little more water if necessary.

Whisk the balsamic vinegar and olive oil in a small bowl until combined.

Divide the figs among serving plates and add a dollop or two of the cheese mixture in between the slices. Sprinkle with walnuts and watercress sprigs and drizzle with the dressing and honey.

Serves 4

½ lemon, juiced

8 ripe green or black figs, stems removed and sliced

150 g mascarpone

150 g gorgonzola dolce (soft, sweet blue cheese), chopped

2 tablespoons aged balsamic vinegar

2 tablespoons extra virgin olive oil

1 handful toasted walnuts, chopped

watercress leaves, to serve

4 tablespoons honey

> Chickpeas with silverbeet and lemon

When chickpeas are cooked properly, they are delicious and readily absorb other flavours. They're wonderful with cinnamon, lemon, garlic and fresh herbs. Serve this with spiced roast lamb or chicken and fetta or yoghurt.

Bring a medium saucepan of water to the boil, add the chickpeas and cinnamon sticks and cook over medium heat for 1–1½ hours or until the chickpeas are tender. Drain and discard the cinnamon sticks. Set the chickpeas aside and remove any loose skins.

Heat the oil in a deep frying pan over low heat and cook the onion and garlic for 10 minutes. Season with salt and pepper, add the silverbeet and cook for a further 20 minutes. Add the chickpeas and parsley and cook for 5 minutes.

Stir in the dill, lemon juice and lemon triangles. Check the seasoning, and serve hot or at room temperature with the lemon wedges.

Serves 6

250 g dried chickpeas, soaked overnight in cold water and drained

2 cinnamon sticks

100 ml extra virgin olive oil

1 small brown onion, finely sliced

3 cloves garlic, finely chopped

sea salt and freshly ground black pepper

1 bunch silverbeet (Swiss chard), trimmed and finely shredded

3 handfuls flat-leaf parsley leaves

3 sprigs dill, chopped

1 lemon, juiced, plus ½ lemon, thinly sliced and cut into triangles

lemon wedges, to serve

PASTA & RICE

Stracci pasta with calamari, radicchio and king brown mushrooms
If time is short, you can substitute bought pasta, such as pappardelle. Use oyster
mushrooms if you can't find the king brown.

Pasta
300 g (10 1/2 oz) [CHECK QUANTITY WITH KAREN – SIDE OF RECIPE WAS CUT
OFF] plain (all-purpose) flour
120 g (4 1/4 oz) fine semolina
pinch of sea salt
4 free-range eggs
1 tablespoon olive oil

100 ml (3 1/2 fl oz) olive oil
150 g (5 1/2 oz) king brown mushrooms, thickly sliced
3 cloves garlic, thinly sliced
4 golden shallots, thinly sliced
2 small red chillies, finely sliced
500 g (1 lb 2 oz) cleaned calamari (squid) with tentacles, cut into thin strips and
tentacles halved
1/2 bunch flat-leaf parsley, coarsely chopped
150 ml (5 fl oz) white wine
1 radicchio heart, shredded
200 ml (7 fl oz) chicken stock (see page xx)
100 g (3 1/2 oz) unsalted butter, chopped
sea salt and freshly ground black pepper
1/2 lemon, juiced
lemon wedges, to serve (optional)

Serves 4–6

To make the pasta, place the flour, semolina and salt in a food processor. Whisk the
eggs and olive oil in a small bowl and add to the processor. Process until the mixture
just forms a ball. Remove and knead lightly, then wrap in plastic film and place in the
fridge for 30 minutes.

Roll the pasta through a pasta machine on the thickest setting and then continue rolling
and changing settings until the pasta is of a good consistency down to the thinnest
setting. Tear it into wide strips. Set aside to rest on a lightly floured tea towel.

Heat the olive oil in a large heavy-based frying pan over medium heat. Add the
mushrooms and cook for 5 minutes. Stir in the garlic, shallots, chilli and calamari, then
add the parsley and wine and cook until the wine has evaporated.

Meanwhile, cook the pasta in plenty of lightly salted water for 4–5 minutes or until al
dente. Drain. Add the pasta, radicchio and stock to mushroom mixture and stir over
medium heat. Add the butter, salt and pepper and lemon juice and stir until the sauce is
glossy and heated through. Serve immediately with lemon wedges, if using.

PASTA
+ 2 rice dishes

Stracci pasta with calamari, radicchio and king brown mushrooms

I love this light pasta dish, with its unusual combination of ingredients. If time is short, you can substitute bought pasta, such as pappardelle. Use oyster mushrooms if you can't find the king brown.

To make the pasta, place the flour, semolina and salt in a food processor. Whisk the eggs and olive oil in a small bowl and add to the processor. Process until the mixture just forms a ball. Remove and knead lightly, then wrap in plastic film and place in the fridge for about 30 minutes.

Roll the pasta through a pasta machine on the thickest setting and then continue rolling until the pasta is of a good consistency, gradually changing settings down to the thinnest setting. Tear it into wide strips. Set aside to rest on a lightly floured tea towel.

Heat the olive oil in a large heavy-based frying pan over medium heat. Add the mushrooms and cook for 5 minutes. Stir in the garlic, shallots, chilli and calamari, then add the parsley and wine and cook until the wine has evaporated.

Meanwhile, cook the pasta in plenty of lightly salted water for 4–5 minutes or until al dente. Drain. Add the pasta, radicchio and stock to the mushroom mixture and stir over medium heat. Add the butter, salt, pepper and lemon juice and stir until the sauce is glossy and heated through. Serve immediately.

Serves 4–6

100 ml olive oil
150 g king brown mushrooms, thickly sliced
3 cloves garlic, thinly sliced
4 golden shallots, thinly sliced
2 small red chillies, finely sliced
500 g cleaned calamari with tentacles, cut into thin strips and tentacles halved
½ bunch flat-leaf parsley, coarsely chopped
150 ml white wine
1 radicchio heart, shredded
200 ml chicken stock (see page 134)
100 g unsalted butter, chopped
sea salt and freshly ground black pepper
½ lemon, juiced

Pasta
300 g plain flour
120 g fine semolina
pinch of sea salt
4 free-range eggs
1 tablespoon olive oil

Orecchiette with cauliflower, anchovies, chilli and garlic

This thick sauce, made in true Roman style, is perfect with short pasta. You can use broccoli instead of the cauliflower to make a beautiful green sauce that is equally irresistible.

Cook the cauliflower in lightly salted boiling water for 15 minutes or until very soft. Drain.

Cook the pasta in lightly salted boiling water until al dente. Drain.

Meanwhile, heat 50 ml olive oil in a medium frying pan and fry the bread slices until crisp and golden. When cool, break into small pieces.

Heat the remaining olive oil in a large saucepan over low heat until hot. Add the garlic, chilli and anchovies and cook for 2–4 minutes. Add the oregano and cauliflower and mash to a coarse paste with the back of a wooden spoon. Season with salt and pepper, then add the cooked pasta and grana padano. Stir to coat, adding more oil if desired. Top with the crispy bread pieces and serve immediately.

Serves 4

1 small cauliflower, cut into quarters
500 g orecchiette pasta
150 ml extra virgin olive oil, plus extra to finish
6 thin slices baguette
4 cloves garlic, finely sliced
2 teaspoons finely chopped fresh chilli
5 anchovy fillets, finely chopped
4 sprigs oregano, leaves only
sea salt and freshly ground black pepper
120 g grated grana padano cheese (see glossary)

Roasted tomato sauce

Use this delicious tomato sauce to make a mean bolognaise or tasty tacos. Or add peas, fresh herbs and parmesan (or pecorino or even goat's cheese) and stir it through your favourite pasta.

Preheat the oven to 170°C. Combine the tomato, shallots, garlic, thyme, oregano, salt, pepper and tomatoes in a large baking dish. Toss to combine and drizzle with the olive oil. Roast for 1½ hours, turning the tomatoes occasionally.

Spoon the mixture into a very large bowl and stir in the water and extra olive oil. Transfer the mixture to a food processor (or use a hand-held mixer) and blend to form a chunky sauce (this may need to be done in batches). Do not strain.

The sauce will keep in the fridge for 5 days, or it can be frozen for up to 3 months.

Makes about 8 cups

2.5 kg very ripe roma tomatoes, cored and
   coarsely chopped
10 golden shallots, coarsely chopped
12 large cloves garlic, finely sliced
¼ bunch thyme, leaves chopped
¼ bunch oregano, leaves chopped
sea salt and freshly ground black pepper
400 g can crushed tomatoes
125 ml extra virgin olive oil
100 ml water
100 ml extra virgin olive oil, extra

Fried rice with egg and ginger

I have simplified this dish by using only the ingredients that I like best. This way, fried rice is less overpowering and can accompany more dishes. Team it with braised honey, soy and ginger spare ribs (see page 174) for an easy Asian dinner.

Place the rice and 4 cups water in a large saucepan over medium heat. Bring to the boil and cook for 10–12 minutes or until tender. Drain, then spread on a tray to cool.

Heat half the oil in a large frying pan or wok over low heat. Add the onion, garlic and ginger, stir for 3 minutes, then remove from the pan. Add the remaining oil and cook the egg until just set. Remove and chop coarsely.

Return the onion mixture to the pan with the rice, soy sauce and sesame oil and stir until the rice is hot. Add the egg, green onion and bean sprouts and stir to combine. Check the seasoning, add more soy sauce if necessary and serve.

Serves 6

2 cups long-grain rice
100 ml vegetable oil
2 large brown onions, sliced
2 cloves garlic, finely chopped
6 cm piece fresh ginger, chopped
4 free-range eggs, lightly beaten
2½ tablespoons light soy sauce
3 drops of sesame oil
½ bunch green onions, finely sliced
250 g bean sprouts

Pasticcio of farfalle

This is my grandmother's recipe. She used to cook up a big batch every week so that there was always plenty on hand. It freezes really well – simply defrost, then reheat it in the oven until it is crispy all over. I like to serve it on top of warmed tomato passata with a green salad.

Cook the pasta in plenty of lightly salted boiling water until al dente. Drain.

Preheat the oven to 170°C. Heat 3 tablespoons olive oil in a large frying pan over medium heat and cook the mince for 6 minutes or until brown. Season the mince and remove from the pan. Add the onion and garlic and cook over high heat for 4 minutes. Stir in the cooked mince, parsley and nutmeg.

Place the cooked pasta in a large bowl and add the mince mixture, peas, grana padano, cream and egg. Season, then add the remaining olive oil to taste, if desired, and stir to combine. Spoon into a large baking dish and press with the back of a spoon. Sprinkle with extra grana padano and bake, covered with foil, for 30 minutes. Remove the foil and bake for 20 minutes more or until golden and crisp.

Serves 6–8

500 g farfalle pasta

3–4 tablespoons extra virgin olive oil

300 g veal or beef mince

sea salt and freshly ground black pepper

1 brown onion, finely chopped

5 cloves garlic, finely chopped

1 bunch flat-leaf parsley, leaves only

1 teaspoon finely grated nutmeg

½ cup fresh or frozen peas

200 g grated grana padano cheese (see glossary), plus 3 tablespoons extra

350 ml pouring cream

4 free-range eggs, lightly beaten

Paella with chicken, prawns, chorizo and capsicum

This is my favourite paella recipe. The best way to cook it is with a few friends in the kitchen and an opened bottle of fino sherry (remember to save some for the paella!).

Heat half the olive oil in a large deep frying pan or a 50 cm paella pan over high heat, add the chicken and cook for 4 minutes. Add the prawns, half the paprika and half the chilli powder and stir for 1 minute. Add the sherry, stir well, then transfer the chicken mixture to a bowl.

Heat the remaining oil in the pan over medium heat and cook the chorizo for 2 minutes, then add the chilli, garlic and onion and cook for 6 minutes. Stir in the remaining paprika and chilli powder and season with salt and pepper. Add the roasted capsicum and rice and stir for 3 minutes, then add the stock and stir well. Simmer over low heat for 10 minutes, then return the chicken mixture to the pan and add the peas and a little more stock, if necessary. Cover and cook over low heat for 1 minute, then rest, covered, for 5 minutes.

Scatter with coriander and mint leaves and serve with lemon wedges.

Serves 6

100 ml olive oil

2 chicken thigh fillets, skin removed, cut into 2 cm pieces

6 green (raw) prawns, peeled and deveined, with heads and tails intact

1 teaspoon smoked paprika

1 teaspoon sweet paprika

½ teaspoon chilli powder

100 ml fino sherry

200 g chorizo sausage, sliced

3 green chillies, seeded and chopped

6 cloves garlic, chopped

2 large red onions, chopped

sea salt and freshly ground black pepper

2 red capsicums (peppers), roasted in a 200°C oven for 25 minutes, then peeled and chopped

350 g calasparra or arborio rice

1.5 litres hot chicken stock (see page 134)

½ cup frozen peas, defrosted

handful coriander leaves

handful mint leaves

2 lemons, cut into wedges

Risi e bisi

This Venetian specialty is traditionally served when the first peas of the season arrive at the markets, and is more like a soup than a risotto. Using sugar snaps for a sweet pea stock is perfect for our Australian climate.

Place the sugar snaps in a large saucepan with the salt flakes and sugar and cover with 1.5 litres water. Bring to the boil, then simmer for 10 minutes until the sugar snaps are tender. Drain, reserving the liquid.

Place the sugar snaps and a little of the cooking water in a food processor and process to a rough pulp. Push through a coarse strainer and return the strained pulp to the cooking liquid.

Heat the butter in a clean saucepan and cook the pancetta, onion, fennel seeds and bay leaf for about 2 minutes. Add the rice and cook for 3 minutes, then pour in the cooking liquid and simmer for 12 minutes. Stir in the peas and parsley and cook for 3 minutes. Season, add a drizzle of olive oil and serve with freshly grated parmesan.

Serves 4

900 g sugar snap peas, cleaned
2 teaspoons sea salt flakes
2 teaspoons sugar
30 g butter
2 cm chunk pancetta, thickly sliced
1 small brown onion, finely diced
1 teaspoon fennel seeds
1 fresh bay leaf
225 g risotto rice
200 g peas, shelled
4 sprigs flat-leaf parsley, leaves only
sea salt and freshly ground black pepper
extra virgin olive oil, for drizzling
grated parmesan, to serve

Pasta with bacon, ricotta, radicchio, chilli and garlic

This recipe is a spin-off of the classic carbonara sauce made from eggs and bacon. I've used ricotta instead of eggs, and the bitter radicchio leaves give the sauce a lift.

Cook the pasta in plenty of lightly salted boiling water until al dente. Drain.

Meanwhile, heat the olive oil in a large frying pan over medium heat and cook the bacon for 2 minutes. Add the shallots, garlic and chillies and cook for 2–3 minutes. Stir in the oregano and wine. Add the cooked pasta, radicchio, ricotta and parsley and stir until the radicchio leaves are wilted. Season to taste and serve drizzled with extra olive oil, if desired.

Serves 4

500 g trofie, strozzapreti or other short, twisted pasta
4 tablespoons extra virgin olive oil
4 thick rashers bacon, coarsely chopped
2 golden shallots, sliced
4 cloves garlic, finely sliced
4 small red chillies, finely chopped
2 tablespoons chopped oregano
100 ml white wine
2 cups torn radicchio leaves
250 g ricotta
2 handfuls chopped flat-leaf parsley
sea salt and freshly ground black pepper
4 tablespoons olive oil, extra (optional)

Pasta with confit of zucchini, peas, garlic and spinach

Zucchini cooked this way takes on a rich, buttery, more intense flavour. Combined with fresh peas, spinach and a touch of cream, it makes a delicious sauce. Recipe pictured following pages.

Cook the pasta in plenty of lightly salted boiling water until al dente. Drain.

Meanwhile, place 100 ml olive oil in a large heavy-based saucepan over medium heat. Add the garlic and some salt, cook for 2 minutes, then reduce the heat to very low and add the zucchini. Cook, stirring occasionally, for about 40 minutes or until the zucchini is golden and soft.

Stir in the wine, peas and spinach. Add the cooked pasta, chilli, cream and remaining olive oil, stir and season to taste with salt and pepper. Serve sprinkled with pecorino.

Serves 4

400 g fresh chitarra pasta or long, thin pasta
  such as spaghettini or linguine
125 ml extra virgin olive oil
4 large cloves garlic, finely sliced
sea salt and freshly ground black pepper
6 zucchini (courgettes), cut into 3 cm slices
2–3 tablespoons white wine
½ cup fresh or frozen peas
3 handfuls baby spinach, shredded
1 small red chilli, finely sliced
4 tablespoons pouring cream
120 g grated pecorino cheese (see glossary)

Pasta with confit of zucchini,
peas, garlic and spinach (see page 85)

Duck and egg fried rice

This is the easiest dinner. Pick up a barbecued duck, a few servings of steamed rice, Chinese pickles and roasted chilli oil from Chinatown on your way home and you have a meal in less than 20 minutes that beats traditional takeaway hands down.

To make the chilli sauce, combine all the ingredients in a small bowl.

Heat the olive oil in a wok or large frying pan over medium heat and cook the garlic and onion until golden. Add the duck skin and meat and stir until hot. Remove from the wok, leaving a little oil behind, and set aside.

Lightly whisk the eggs, then add to the wok over high heat and cook to make an omelette. Remove and cut into strands when cool enough to handle. Add the rice to the wok and break up with a wooden spoon. Add 1 tablespoon water, any duck juices, the bean sprouts, snake beans, green onion and half the coriander. Cook for 1 minute over high heat, then add the duck and omelette and stir until heated through.

Spoon the fried rice into bowls and top with Chinese pickles and the remaining coriander. Serve with the chilli sauce.

Serves 4–6

160 ml olive oil

6 cloves garlic, sliced

1 brown onion, sliced

1 cold barbecued duck, skin and meat removed and roughly chopped, and any juices reserved

4 large free-range eggs

6 servings bought steamed rice

2 handfuls bean sprouts

8 snake beans, cut into 2 cm slices and blanched

12 green onions, sliced

8 sprigs coriander

1 cup Chinese pickles (available from Asian food stores and restaurants)

Chilli sauce

2 tablespoons bought roasted chilli oil

3 small red chillies, finely chopped (or to taste)

3 tablespoons light soy sauce

4 drops of sesame oil

< Pappardelle with duck and mandarin ragu

Wonderfully fragrant, mandarins add a refreshing tang to both sweet and savoury dishes. To get the best results, braise the duck meat slowly – don't rush it.

Preheat the oven to 240°C. Season the duck pieces with salt and pepper, place on an oven rack and roast for 15 minutes.

Heat the olive oil in a large saucepan over medium heat and cook the onion, garlic, leek and bay leaf for 2–3 minutes. Add the mandarin zest and carrot and cook for 15 minutes, stirring frequently. Add the thyme, verjuice, duck pieces and mandarin juice and simmer for 5 minutes, then pour in the stock and simmer over medium heat for a further 40 minutes or until the duck is very tender and the sauce has reduced.

Remove the duck and cut the meat into bite-sized pieces while still warm. Return to the ragu and check the seasoning.

Cook the pappardelle in plenty of lightly salted boiling water for about 3–4 minutes or until al dente. Drain. Add the pasta to the ragu and stir to combine. Stir in the parsley and serve with freshly grated parmesan, if using.

Serves 6

4 duck maryland (leg and thigh portions),
　trimmed and halved
sea salt and freshly ground black pepper
3 tablespoons extra virgin olive oil
1 brown onion, halved and sliced
6 cloves garlic, chopped
1 leek, trimmed and finely sliced
1 fresh bay leaf
finely grated zest and juice of 3 mandarins
1 carrot, finely chopped
5 sprigs thyme
400 ml verjuice (see glossary)
2 litres chicken stock (see page 134)
500 g fresh or dried pappardelle
6 sprigs flat-leaf parsley, leaves only
grated parmesan, to serve (optional)

Linguine with mushrooms and bacon

Dried porcini mushrooms give this dish a flavour boost and an irresistible heady aroma.

Cook the linguine in plenty of lightly salted boiling water until al dente. Drain, reserving 1 cup of the cooking liquid.

Heat 1 tablespoon olive oil in a large frying pan and cook the bacon over medium heat until crisp. Add the mushrooms and cook for 5 minutes. Add another tablespoon oil, then stir in the garlic, porcini and chilli. Pour in the wine and stir to deglaze the pan.

Add the reserved cooking liquid to the bacon mixture, then stir in the cooked pasta, parsley, butter and remaining oil. Season with salt and pepper and serve in warm bowls with parmesan.

Serves 4

400 g linguine
4 tablespoons olive oil
4 rashers rindless bacon, chopped
8 Swiss brown mushrooms, sliced
2 cloves garlic, finely chopped
1 tablespoon porcini powder (see glossary)
　or 2 tablespoons dried porcini mushrooms,
　soaked, drained and chopped
2 green chillies, finely sliced
200 ml white wine
5 sprigs parsley, leaves chopped
150 g unsalted butter, chopped
sea salt and freshly ground black pepper
grated parmesan, to serve

Spaghettini and meatballs

I think everybody has a soft spot for meatballs, and it's always fun to get everyone involved in making them. Comfort food at its best.

To make the tomato sauce, heat the olive oil in a very large saucepan over medium heat. Cook the garlic until golden, then add the bay leaf and oregano and cook for 1 minute. Add the tomatoes and passata and simmer for 10 minutes, then stir in the sugar and chicken stock and season to taste. Simmer over low heat for 20 minutes.

To make the meatballs, heat the olive oil in a large frying pan over medium heat. Add the onion, garlic and oregano and season with salt and pepper. Cook for 3–5 minutes or until the onion is soft.

Place the remaining ingredients (except the extra olive oil) in a food processor, add the onion mixture and pulse until well combined. Form the mince mixture into small balls about the size of a walnut.

Heat the extra oil in a large frying pan over medium heat. Brown the meatballs in batches, then add to the tomato sauce and simmer over low heat for 15–20 minutes.

Meanwhile, cook the spaghettini in a very large saucepan of lightly salted water until al dente. Drain. Stir the pasta and peas through the sauce and serve hot with grated parmesan.

Serves 8–10

800 g spaghettini
½ cup frozen peas
grated parmesan, to serve

Meatballs
2 tablespoons olive oil, plus extra for frying
2 brown onions, chopped
6 cloves garlic, finely chopped
1 handful chopped oregano
sea salt and freshly ground black pepper
450 g pork and veal sausages, skins removed
350 g beef mince
200 g grated parmesan
2 free-range eggs
100 g freshly made breadcrumbs
½ fresh nutmeg, grated
handful flat-leaf parsley, chopped

Tomato sauce
100 ml olive oil
2 cloves garlic, finely sliced
1 bay leaf
1 handful oregano leaves
2 × 400 g cans chopped tomatoes
2¾ cups tomato passata
2 tablespoons castor sugar
500 ml chicken stock (see page 134)

< Tagliatelle with shaved parsnip, pancetta and sage

Parsnip makes a perfect partner for pancetta. It's sweet and nutty and, when shaved, crisps beautifully. Don't forget the lemon juice in this recipe – it gives the rich, creamy sauce a zesty jolt.

Cook the pasta in plenty of lightly salted boiling water until al dente. Drain.

Use a vegetable peeler to cut the parsnips into fine shavings (discarding the fibrous centre).

Heat half the oil in a large, deep frying pan over high heat and cook the pancetta slices until browned and crispy. Add the garlic, sage, chilli and parsnip shavings and remaining oil (if necessary) and cook until the parsnip is crisp.

Pour in the wine and cook for 2 minutes, then add the cream. Add the cooked pasta and a little water if necessary, then toss to combine. Add the parmesan and lemon juice, season with salt and pepper and serve in warm pasta bowls.

Serves 2

260 g tagliatelle
1 parsnip, peeled
3 tablespoons extra virgin olive oil
8 slices spicy pancetta (see glossary)
2 garlic cloves, finely sliced
2 handfuls sage leaves
1 teaspoon dried chilli flakes
100 ml white wine
150 ml pouring cream
50 g shaved parmesan
1 tablespoon lemon juice
sea salt and freshly ground black pepper

Rigatoni with roasted cauliflower, saffron, currants, pine nuts and caramelised onion

Roasting the cauliflower for this southern Italian-style pasta makes all the difference. It's a terrific combination of flavours.

Preheat the oven to 200°C. Cut the cauliflower into florets, brush with some of the olive oil and roast for 25 minutes or until golden.

Cook the pasta in lightly salted boiling water until al dente. Drain.

Heat the remaining olive oil in a large saucepan over very low heat until hot. Add the onion, garlic and thyme and cook for 25 minutes.

Meanwhile, place the currants and vinegar in a small saucepan and bring to the boil. Remove from the heat and drain.

Stir the anchovies into the onion mixture and season with salt and pepper. Add the currants, cauliflower, saffron and ½ cup water and simmer for 5 minutes. Add the pine nuts, extra olive oil, extra vinegar, wine and cooked pasta and stir over low heat for 5 minutes. Check the seasoning, then add the parmesan and parsley. Toss to combine and serve immediately.

Serves 4

1 small cauliflower
125 ml extra virgin olive oil, plus 1 tablespoon extra
500 g rigatoni
2 brown onions, sliced
4 cloves garlic, sliced
3 sprigs thyme
80 g currants
100 ml red wine vinegar, plus 1 tablespoon extra
3 anchovy fillets, chopped
sea salt and freshly ground black pepper
2 pinches of saffron threads
70 g pine nuts
200 ml white wine
120 g grated parmesan
6 sprigs flat-leaf parsley, leaves coarsely chopped

Risotto with taleggio
and rosemary (see page 98)

Risotto with taleggio and rosemary

Taleggio is a delicious washed-rind cow's milk cheese that melts beautifully. A little of this rich, creamy risotto, spiked with the heady scent of rosemary, goes a long way. Recipe pictured previous pages.

Heat the chicken stock in a large saucepan over medium heat until simmering.

Heat the olive oil in a large heavy-based saucepan over low heat and cook the shallots and garlic for 5 minutes or until soft. Add the rice, rosemary and bay leaf and stir over low heat for about 3 minutes or until the rice is coated with oil and lightly toasted. Add the wine and stir over medium heat for about 5 minutes or until the liquid is absorbed.

Add 1 cup simmering stock to the rice and stir over medium heat for 5 minutes or until the stock is absorbed. Add the remaining stock, half a cup at a time, and stir continuously, allowing each addition to be absorbed before adding the next. This should take about 20 minutes.

When the rice is almost cooked and you have about a cup of stock left, stir in the taleggio and butter, a few pieces at a time. Season to taste with salt and pepper, stir in the parmesan and serve immediately.

Serves 6

1.5 litres chicken stock (see page 134)
1½ tablespoons olive oil
5 golden shallots, chopped
3 cloves garlic, finely sliced
500 g arborio rice
2 sprigs rosemary, leaves finely chopped
1 bay leaf
100 ml white wine
120 g taleggio cheese (see glossary), torn into pieces
80 g unsalted butter, chopped
sea salt and freshly ground black pepper
150 g grated parmesan

> Pennette with prawns and fennel

The great flavour of this dish comes from cooking the prawn heads in the oil first. I actually leave the heads in to serve so I can suck every last drop of juice out of them.

Bring a large saucepan of salted water to the boil and cook the fennel wedges for 10 minutes or until tender. Drain and chop into bite-sized chunks.

Cook the pasta in a large saucepan of salted water for 7–9 minutes or until al dente.

Remove the heads from the prawns and reserve, then peel the prawns. Remove the vein and chop the prawn meat into small pieces.

Heat most of the oil in a large frying pan. Add the prawn heads, season well and cook for 2 minutes, squashing the juices out of the heads to stain the oil. Add the chopped prawn meat and cook for 1 minute, then add the garlic and chilli and fry for 2 minutes. Stir in the fennel and check the seasoning.

Drain the pasta and toss straight into the frying pan. Add the butter and remaining oil and cook for 1 minute to allow the pasta to absorb some of the juices. Serve immediately.

Serves 4

1 large bulb fennel, cut into wedges, any green tops chopped
500 g pennette pasta
12 large green (raw) tiger prawns
120 ml extra virgin olive oil
sea salt and freshly ground black pepper
3 cloves garlic, sliced
1 teaspoon dried chilli flakes
80 g butter

Pan-fried rainbow trout with almonds and garlic butter

This is an elegant way to serve whole fish that's an easy and quick dinner for two for any night of the week. Serve with salad and boiled chat potatoes or mash.

Heat the oil in a large frying pan over medium–high heat. Season the trout with salt and pepper and cook for 3 minutes or until browned, then turn and cook for a further 3–4 minutes or until just cooked through. Remove and keep warm.

Drain any excess oil from the pan, then melt the butter until bubbling. Add the almonds, parsley, garlic and capers. Check the seasoning and add the lemon juice. Spoon the sauce over the fish and serve with lemon wedges.

Serves 2

1½ tablespoons oil
2 whole rainbow trout (you can use fillets)
sea salt and freshly ground black pepper
120 g unsalted butter, chopped
3–4 tablespoons slivered almonds, toasted
6 sprigs flat-leaf parsley, leaves chopped
2 cloves garlic, finely chopped
4 tablespoons capers
1 lemon, juiced
lemon wedges, to serve

> Spice-dusted barramundi with Moroccan herb salad

I grew up eating fish cooked this way, and the accompanying salad is based on one my grandmother used to make. Cutlets of fish, cut across the bone, are great to cook with as the fish stays delicious and moist. And don't worry – the bones are large enough to pick out easily once cooked.

For the salad, combine all the ingredients in a bowl and mix well.

Combine the cumin, coriander, salt, pepper, chilli flakes and flour in a large plastic bag and mix well.

Heat the oil to 180°C in a large saucepan or deep-fryer. Place the cutlets in the plastic bag and shake gently to coat with the spice mixture. Remove and shake off any excess. Fry the cutlets in the hot oil for 5–8 minutes or until just cooked. Serve topped with the herb salad and lemon cheeks.

Serves 4

2 tablespoons ground cumin
2 teaspoons ground coriander
2 tablespoons sea salt
¼ teaspoon freshly ground black pepper
2 tablespoons dried chilli flakes
½ cup plain flour
canola oil, for deep-frying
4 barramundi cutlets (about 200 g each)
lemon cheeks, to serve

Moroccan herb salad

2 tablespoons drained capers, chopped
½ bunch flat-leaf parsley, leaves roughly chopped
1 small bunch coriander, leaves roughly chopped
1 lemon, zest finely grated, plus segments from 1 lemon, coarsely chopped
4 green onions, sliced diagonally
2 teaspoons finely chopped preserved lemon rind (optional)

Baked scallops with cannellini-bean puree and sage and lemon burnt-butter sauce

Fresh scallops are such an indulgence, yet so easy to cook. The secret's in the timing so have everything ready to go.

Preheat the oven to 220°C. Detach the scallops from the shells with a small sharp knife and trim if necessary. Place on a large baking tray and season well with salt and pepper. Drizzle with a little of the olive oil.

Place the cannellini beans in a saucepan, add 300 ml water and bring to the boil over medium heat. Simmer for 3 minutes, then drain and coarsely mash with a fork, leaving some whole. Add the remaining olive oil and half the lemon juice, season with salt and pepper and stir well.

Bake the scallops for 3–4 minutes or until just opaque. Transfer to a serving platter and spoon the cannellini-bean puree over the top.

Melt the butter in a frying pan over medium heat, season and when hot, add the garlic and fry for 1 minute or until fragrant. Add the sage leaves and cook over high heat for 2–3 minutes or until the butter is brown. Remove from the heat and stir in the remaining lemon juice. Spoon the sauce over the scallops and serve immediately with lemon wedges.

Serves 4

12 jumbo scallops on the half shell
sea salt and freshly ground black pepper
2½ tablespoons extra virgin olive oil
400 g can cannellini beans, drained
1 lemon, juiced
80 g unsalted butter
1 clove garlic, very finely sliced
20 sage leaves, large ones torn
lemon wedges, to serve

Swordfish with tomato, chilli and caper sauce

The flavours of the Mediterranean – garlic, olives, capers and chilli – are exquisite with swordfish. This fleshy tomato-based sauce can be made ahead of time and will keep for three days in the fridge.

Heat the olive oil in a large saucepan over medium heat. Cook the garlic for 1–2 minutes or until golden, then add the caperberries or capers, olives, chilli flakes and salt to taste. Pour in the wine and bring to the boil. Add the tomato sauce and simmer over low heat for about 5 minutes. Check the seasoning and stir in the basil.

Brush the swordfish with olive oil and season with salt and pepper. Heat a large non-stick frying pan over high heat and sear the fish for about 2 minutes each side or until just cooked.

Spoon the sauce onto four plates or a large platter and top with the fish. Scatter with the extra basil and serve with a green salad and crusty bread.

Serves 4

200 ml extra virgin olive oil, plus extra for brushing
4 cloves garlic, finely sliced
7 caperberries, drained and sliced or 2 tablespoons capers, drained
4 tablespoons black olives, pitted
1 teaspoon dried chilli flakes
sea salt and freshly ground black pepper
200 ml white wine
3 cups chunky tomato pasta sauce
2 handfuls basil leaves, plus extra to serve
4 swordfish fillets (about 120 g each and 2 cm thick), cut in half lengthways

Blue swimmer crab and corn fluffy omelette

This is perfect for a weekend brunch or as a starter. Alternatively, you could increase the recipe to make a large omelette for a bigger group. Recipe pictured following pages.

Preheat the oven to 200°C. Whisk the egg whites and salt in a large bowl until stiff peaks form. Mix the egg yolks, fish sauce and pepper in a separate bowl, then fold in the egg whites until just combined.

Heat a non-stick ovenproof frying pan over high heat for 1 minute. Add the butter and, when melted, pour in the egg mixture and sprinkle with cheese, crabmeat and corn kernels. Cook for 1 minute, then transfer the pan to the oven. Bake for about 5 minutes or until cooked to your liking.

For the snow pea shoot salad, combine the chilli, coriander, chives, green onion and snow pea shoots. Add the lime juice and fish sauce to taste.

Slide the omelette onto a warm plate for a shared meal, or halve the omelette and place on two plates. Top with the snow pea shoot salad and serve immediately.

Serves 2

3 free-range eggs, separated
pinch of sea salt
4 drops of fish sauce
freshly ground black pepper
2 knobs unsalted butter
80 g grated cheddar or gruyère cheese
150 g cooked blue swimmer crabmeat (available from fishmongers – you may need to order it in advance)
1 cob corn, cooked and kernels removed

Snow pea shoot salad
1 green chilli, finely sliced
2 sprigs coriander
¼ bunch chives, snipped
2 green onions, finely sliced
2 handfuls snow pea shoots
1 lime, juiced
fish sauce, to taste

Blue swimmer crab and corn
fluffy omelette (see page 105)

Smoked eel and ruby grapefruit salad

This salad is an unusual take on the prawn cocktail, and should be assembled just before serving. Serve it in chilled martini glasses as a fancy appetiser at a formal dinner party.

Place the egg, mayonnaise, yoghurt and cayenne in a small bowl and stir. Season with salt and pepper, then spoon into four glasses.

Place the endive sprigs, grapefruit and chives in a medium bowl and mix gently to combine. Divide among the glasses and place the smoked eel or trout on top. Drizzle with lemon juice, sprinkle with pepper and scatter with chervil leaves and fried shallots. Serve immediately.

Serves 4

3 free-range eggs, hard-boiled and chopped
½ cup good-quality mayonnaise
½ cup thick plain yoghurt
2 pinches of cayenne pepper
sea salt and freshly ground black pepper
1 endive, curly sprigs only
2 ruby grapefruit, peeled and segmented
4 tablespoons chopped chives
500 g smoked eel, flesh cleaned and skin and bones
   removed, then cut into 3 cm dice, or 500 g smoked
   trout, skin and bones removed, then flaked into
   large chunks
½ lemon, juiced
¼ bunch chervil, leaves only
2 tablespoons fried shallots (available from Asian
   food stores)

Seared sardines with onions, parsley and currants

Prepared in this agrodolce (sweet and sour) style, sardines make a great snack. If you have never really liked sardines, this dish may just convert you.

Season the sardines with salt and pepper. Heat 1 tablespoon olive oil in a large non-stick frying pan over medium heat. Add the onion and garlic and cook, stirring occasionally, for 5 minutes or until the onion is soft. Transfer to a bowl.

Heat 1 tablespoon olive oil in frying pan over high heat. Add half the sardines, skin-side down, and cook for 2–4 minutes or until the sardines just change colour. Remove and place skin-side down on a serving platter. Repeat with the remaining sardines.

Whisk the red wine vinegar with the remaining olive oil in a small bowl. Season and add the onion mixture, currants, pine nuts and parsley. Mix well, then pour the dressing over the sardines. Serve warm.

Serves 10–12 as an antipasto

12 fresh sardine fillets, butterflied
sea salt and freshly ground black pepper
100 ml extra virgin olive oil
1 large red onion, halved and sliced
3 cloves garlic, finely chopped
4 tablespoons red wine vinegar
3 tablespoons currants, brought to the boil
   in 4 tablespoons red wine vinegar, then drained
3 tablespoons pine nuts, toasted
4 sprigs flat-leaf parsley, leaves torn

Blue swimmer crab with white and green asparagus salad

You can buy cooked blue swimmer crabmeat from fish markets and fish shops but you may need to order it in advance.

Place the crabmeat in a medium frying pan over low heat. Heat until warm, then transfer to a bowl and season with salt, pepper and a little lemon juice. Keep warm.

Combine the yoghurt, mayonnaise, shallots and egg in a bowl and mix well. Spoon the yoghurt mixture onto a plate, top with avocado and sprinkle with cayenne pepper.

Place the asparagus ribbons in a bowl and drizzle with olive oil and the remaining lemon juice. Toss with the chives.

Arrange the asparagus on top of the avocado and sprinkle with warm crabmeat and chervil. Serve with lemon wedges.

Serves 4 as a starter

400 g cooked blue swimmer crabmeat
sea salt and freshly ground black pepper
1 lemon, juiced
½ cup thick plain yoghurt
3 tablespoons good-quality mayonnaise
2 golden shallots, finely sliced
3 hard-boiled free-range eggs, chopped
1 ripe avocado, chopped
cayenne pepper, to taste
½ bunch each white and green asparagus, ends
   peeled, sliced into thin ribbons with a mandolin or
   vegetable peeler and blanched in salted boiling
   water for 90 seconds
100 ml olive oil
½ bunch chives, finely chopped
1 handful chervil leaves, to serve
lemon wedges, to serve

Flathead fillets in beer batter

After 20 years, I think I've finally perfected my recipe for beer batter. The cornflour helps guarantee a crisp result. Serve the fish with a salad dressed with vinegar or lemon juice to complement the crunchy batter. If you are making chips, use trent potatoes, or try kipfler skins (see page 16). Recipe pictured following pages.

For the batter, combine the flours and salt in a large bowl. Make a well in the centre and gradually add the combined beer and mineral water. Mix to a smooth batter.

Heat the oil in a large saucepan or deep-fryer until very hot (190°C). Dip the fish in the plain flour, then in the batter and deep-fry in batches until golden and cooked through. Drain on paper towels and keep warm.

Fry the parsley sprigs in the hot oil (take care as the oil will spit). Drain on paper towels.

Serve the fish with crisp parsley sprigs and lemon wedges.

Serves 4

cottonseed oil (see glossary), for deep-frying
8–12 flathead fillets (about 100 g each), skin on
plain flour, for dusting
¼ bunch parsley, broken into sprigs
2 lemons, cut into wedges

Beer batter
250 g plain flour
250 g cornflour
1 tablespoon salt
375 ml beer
250 ml sparkling mineral water

Flathead fillets in beer batter
(see page 109)

Kibbeh-style ocean trout

This kibbeh is just superb. If you are a little unsure about raw fish, this may just be the dish to tempt you – it's addictive. Serve as an appetiser with drinks, or in smaller portions as a starter.

Chill a large ceramic or glass bowl, then add the trout, shallots, burghul, sumac (if using), allspice, garlic, salt, pepper, chillies, lemon juice and zest and olive oil. Mix to a paste, then press the mixture onto a flat platter. Drizzle with a little extra olive oil and press plastic film onto the surface to cover. Chill until ready to serve.

Scatter the pickles and mint over the trout mixture. Drizzle with extra olive oil and serve with lemon halves and bread triangles.

Serves 8 as a starter

400 g ocean trout, skin and bones removed, pulsed in a food processor to a medium–fine paste

2 golden shallots, finely chopped

150 g coarse burghul (see glossary), soaked in 185 ml hot water for 10 minutes, then squeezed dry

3 teaspoons sumac (optional; see glossary)

3 pinches of allspice

½ clove garlic, finely chopped

1½ teaspoons salt flakes

freshly ground black pepper

1 large green chilli, seeded and finely chopped

2 large red chillies, seeded and finely chopped

finely grated zest and juice of ½ lemon

3 tablespoons extra virgin olive oil, plus extra for drizzling

4 tablespoons pickled vegetables, finely chopped (see page 19)

3 sprigs mint, leaves only

lemon halves, to serve

4 round flat breads or Turkish bread, cut into triangles, to serve

Warm mussel and leek salad
(see page 116)

Warm mussel and leek salad

It might be an unusual salad but this delicious combination makes a stunning first course. Leeks are available all year round but are at their best from spring to autumn. Recipe pictured opposite and previous pages.

Cook the whole leeks in plenty of lightly salted boiling water over medium heat for about 15–18 minutes or until tender. Remove and drain on paper towels.

Pour the wine into a large saucepan and bring to the boil. Add the mussels and cook, covered, over high heat for 3–4 minutes. Remove the lid, stir and cook for another minute, uncovered. Drain the mussels, reserving the cooking liquid, and discard any unopened ones. Remove some of the mussels from their shells.

Place half the olive oil in a large frying pan over medium heat and cook the shallots and garlic for 5–7 minutes or until the shallots are soft. Add the cumin seeds and stir for 1 minute. Add the strained cooking liquid, increase the heat and boil until reduced by half. Add the cream and simmer for about 3 minutes, until slightly thickened.

Cut the leeks in half and arrange on a serving platter. Scatter the mussels and olives over the top and season with black pepper. Add the parsley, lemon juice and remaining olive oil to the cream mixture and pour over the leeks and mussels. Serve immediately.

Serves 4 as a starter

5 small leeks, trimmed and washed
200 ml sparkling wine
1.5 kg black mussels, scrubbed and beards removed
2½ tablespoons extra virgin olive oil
4 golden shallots, finely sliced
3 cloves garlic, finely chopped
3 teaspoons cumin seeds, toasted and crushed
200 ml pouring cream
10 pitted green olives, chopped
freshly ground black pepper
½ bunch flat-leaf parsley, leaves finely chopped
½ lemon, juiced

Crayfish salad a la Rousse with saffron

This salad, which is served either cold or at room temperature, can be made with cooked crayfish but fresh green crayfish is much tastier. It's perfect for special occasions, and I especially love it at Christmas. For extra decadence, scatter a little caviar over the salad just before serving – Sevruga is wonderful, but expensive.

Bring a large saucepan of salted water to the boil. Add the lemon juice, squeezed lemon half and crayfish and cook over medium heat for 25 minutes. Drain, remove the crayfish from the pan and set aside to cool for 20 minutes.

Use a large knife to cut the crayfish in half lengthways and remove and discard the vein. Remove the crayfish meat, reserving the shells and leaving the tail intact. Chop the meat into chunks and place in a large bowl. Add the peas and cover.

Cook the potato, turnip and carrots in boiling salted water for about 10 minutes or until tender. Drain and cool, then add to the crayfish. Add the hard-boiled eggs and stir to combine.

Process the raw egg yolks, mustard, saffron threads and soaking liquid and garlic paste in a food processor for 1 minute. With the motor running, slowly add the olive oil and process until smooth and thick. Place in a bowl and stir in the lemon juice, yoghurt, salt and pepper. Add the mayonnaise to the crayfish salad and fold it through gently.

To serve, fill the shells with the salad and place on a large platter. Scatter with chives, mint, coriander, witlof, watercress and chilli. Add a squeeze of lemon and a splash of extra virgin olive oil and serve with lemon wedges.

Serves 8 as a starter

½ lemon, juiced

1 large (1.3 kg) live green (raw) crayfish, chilled for 30 minutes in the freezer.

¼ cup frozen peas, blanched in boiling salted water for 1 minute, then drained

4 large kipfler potatoes, sliced

1 turnip, cut into 2 cm pieces

6–8 Dutch (baby) carrots, cut into 2 cm pieces on an angle

2 hard-boiled free-range eggs, peeled and chopped

2 raw free-range egg yolks

1 tablespoon Dijon mustard

2 pinches of saffron threads, soaked in 2½ tablespoons boiling water

1 clove garlic, pounded to a paste with 1½ tablespoons sea salt, or to taste

350 ml extra virgin olive oil, plus extra to serve

lemon juice, to taste

100 g thick plain yoghurt

sea salt and freshly ground black pepper

½ bunch chives, chopped

½ cup mint leaves

½ cup coriander leaves

1 head witlof (Belgian endive), tips only

1 cup watercress sprigs

1 green chilli, seeded and sliced

3 lemons, cut into wedges

Caper and yoghurt sauce

This sauce is so well suited to seafood. It's superb with any grilled, poached or pan-fried fish.

Combine the bread, capers, green onion, parsley, garlic and egg yolk in a blender or food processor and process until smooth. Add the olive oil and yoghurt and process to combine. Season to taste. The sauce will keep in an airtight container in the fridge for up to 2 days.

Makes about 2¹/₂ cups

3 slices stale bread, crusts removed, then soaked in water and squeezed
100 g salted capers, rinsed
1 bunch green onions, blanched and coarsely chopped
¹/₂ bunch flat-leaf parsley, blanched and coarsely chopped
1 clove garlic
1 free-range egg yolk
200 ml extra virgin olive oil
200 g plain yoghurt
sea salt and freshly ground black pepper

Seared scallops with pancetta and cauliflower puree

This is a tasty starter – so easy to prepare ahead of time and it cooks in a flash.

Cook the cauliflower and potato in enough lightly salted boiling water to just cover the vegetables for 15 minutes or until tender. Drain well and transfer to a blender or food processor. With the motor running, add the butter piece by piece until the mixture is smooth. Season with salt and keep warm.

Clean the scallops, discarding any grit and sinew, season with salt and pepper and drizzle with olive oil. Roll each scallop in a slice of pancetta. Heat a frying pan over high heat. When hot, place the scallops in the pan and sear for about 80 seconds on each side, turning once, until the pancetta is crisp. Add the butter and heat until melted, then add the sage leaves and fry for 30 seconds. Pour in the lemon juice.

Dollop warm cauliflower puree on serving plates. Spoon on the scallops, pan juices and sage leaves.

Serves 4 as a starter

¹/₂ cauliflower (including stalk), sliced
1 desiree potato, thinly sliced
75 g unsalted butter, chopped
sea salt

Seared scallops
12 large scallops
sea salt and freshly ground black pepper
2¹/₂ tablespoons olive oil
12 slices pancetta
2 knobs unsalted butter
12 sage leaves
¹/₂ lemon, juiced

Pan-seared yellowfin tuna with smoky eggplant and chilli cherry tomato salad

Rare-seared tuna works really well with this luscious eggplant, which is also great on its own with bread, and the tomato salad gives the dish a zingy lift. Swordfish or marlin also work well in this recipe. Recipe pictured following pages.

Preheat the oven to 180°C. Turn your largest burner on high and rest the eggplants directly on the flames, rotating every 3 minutes until all the sides are blackened (it should take about 9 minutes). Alternatively, cook under a hot grill, turning occasionally, until blackened. Place the eggplant on a baking tray and cook in the oven for 10 minutes. Remove and leave to cool.

Cut the eggplants down the middle and scoop out the soft flesh, leaving the black shell behind. Chop the flesh until you have a chunky paste, draining off any excess liquid as you go. Place in a bowl with the yoghurt, lemon and half the olive oil and combine – the mixture will look a little creamy. Set aside.

Combine all the salad ingredients in a bowl, then cover and leave to marinate.

Rub the remaining olive oil over the tuna steaks and season well. Heat a large, heavy-based frying pan over high heat for about 4 minutes, then sear the tuna for 1–2 minutes on each side. You want the fish to be rare. Take care not to overcook it – tuna at room temperature will cook more quickly than tuna from the fridge.

To serve, spoon some eggplant mixture onto two plates, top with the tuna steaks and serve the salad and juices on the side.

Serves 2

2 large eggplants (aubergines)
2 tablespoons plain yoghurt
½ lemon, juiced
2½ tablespoons extra virgin olive oil
2 × 200 g yellowfin tuna steaks, at room temperature
sea salt and freshly ground black pepper

Chilli cherry tomato salad
¼ red onion, finely diced
½ punnet cherry tomatoes, cut into slices
2 sprigs mint, leaves shredded
¼ teaspoon dried chilli flakes
1 tablespoon red wine vinegar
3 tablespoons extra virgin olive oil

Pan-seared yellowfin tuna with
smoky eggplant and chilli cherry
tomato salad (see page 121)

Baked flathead with roast potatoes, lemon and oregano

The oregano and lemon dressing gives this dish a real zing. If you can't get flathead, whiting or snapper also work well.

Preheat the oven to 185°C. Line a large baking dish with baking paper.

To make the oregano dressing, combine all the ingredients except the lemon juice in a food processor or blender and process to a paste. Stir in the lemon juice.

Combine the potatoes, shallots, garlic, salt, pepper and 2 tablespoons olive oil and arrange in the lined baking dish. Pour the wine over the potatoes and bake for 20 minutes.

Rub the lemon juice and remaining olive oil all over the fish, then season with salt and pepper. Place the lemon slices inside the fish, then place on top of the potato mixture in the baking dish and bake for 20–30 minutes or until the fish are just cooked. Remove and set aside, covered, in a warm place for 10 minutes.

Serve the fish on top of the potatoes and drizzle with oregano dressing.

Serves 2

6 kipfler potatoes, very thinly sliced
3 golden shallots, finely sliced
3 cloves garlic, finely sliced
4 tablespoons salt flakes (or to taste)
10 grinds freshly ground black pepper
4 tablespoons olive oil
100 ml white wine
½ lemon, juiced
2 flathead (about 350 g each), scaled and gutted
1 lemon, sliced

Oregano dressing
finely grated zest of 1 lemon
12 sprigs oregano, leaves picked
8 sprigs flat-leaf parsley
2 small red chillies, finely chopped (or to taste)
100 ml extra virgin olive oil
½ clove garlic
pinch of sea salt
lemon juice, to taste

Crushed olive-oil potatoes and baked flathead with mint and caper dressing

This is a great light lunch. The roughly mashed potato beautifully complements the subtle flavour of the baked fish.

Preheat the oven to 220°C.

Combine all the dressing ingredients in a small bowl and stir well. Set aside to allow the flavours to develop.

Place the fish fillets, skin-side up, on a non-stick baking tray, season with salt and drizzle with 2–3 tablespoons olive oil. Bake for 7–10 minutes (depending on the thickness of the fish) or until just cooked.

Place the potatoes in a shallow bowl and crush with a fork. Add the remaining oil, stir and season well with salt and pepper.

Arrange the warm potatoes on a platter, top with the fish and dressing and serve with lemon wedges on the side.

Serves 4

8 flathead or whiting fillets (about 100 g each), skin on
sea salt and freshly ground black pepper
125 ml extra virgin olive oil
6 desiree potatoes, cut into chunks, boiled until soft, drained and kept warm
lemon wedges, to serve

Mint and caper dressing

2 handfuls mint, leaves finely chopped
2 handfuls flat-leaf parsley, leaves finely chopped
4 tablespoons capers, chopped
1 gherkin, chopped
½ clove garlic, finely chopped
1 green chilli, finely sliced
125 ml extra virgin olive oil
1 lemon, juiced
finely grated zest of ½ lemon
2 golden shallots, finely chopped
3 tablespoons red wine vinegar
freshly ground black pepper

Baked flounder with dried black olive and lemon dressing

So simple and delicious, and I've found this is the best way to cook whole fish without smelling the house out. Just make sure your fish are as fresh as possible. Recipe pictured following pages.

Preheat the oven to 220°C and line a large baking tray with baking paper.

To make the dressing, combine all the ingredients in a small bowl and leave for 15 minutes to the allow the flavours to develop.

Lay the flounder on the prepared tray and stuff with lemon slices and parsley. Season with salt and pepper, drizzle with oil and roast for 20 minutes. Finish under a hot grill for 2 minutes to crisp the skin, then spoon the dressing over the top and serve.

Serves 2

2 whole flounder (about 500 g each), cleaned, pierced with a sharp knife, following the natural edge of the flounder
1 lemon, cut into thin slices
2 sprigs flat-leaf parsley
sea salt and freshly ground black pepper
1 tablespoon extra virgin olive oil

Dried black olive and lemon dressing

75 ml extra virgin olive oil
15 dried black olives, pitted and diced
1 lemon, segmented and chopped
½ clove garlic, sliced
1 small celery heart, finely diced, leaves torn
1 red chilli, finely sliced
sea salt and freshly ground black pepper

Baked flounder with dried black olive and lemon dressing (see page 125)

< Roast garlic prawns in the shell

I always find it hard to go past garlic prawns. This is a different take on the classic dish and is one of my favourite recipes at the moment. I can't stop cooking it! Make sure you have napkins and finger bowls on hand.

Cut down the back of each prawn with a small, sharp knife and remove the intestinal tract, leaving the shell on.

Combine the fennel seeds, peppercorns and salt in a mortar and pestle or blender and grind to a fine powder. Add the garlic and pound to a paste, then add half the olive oil. Pour the marinade and remaining olive oil over the prawns and toss to coat.

Heat a wok over medium heat for 3 minutes. Add the prawns and marinade and cook for 2 minutes. Turn the prawns and cook for a further 2 minutes. Add the wine or sherry and parsley, swirl the pan for 30 seconds, then pour the prawns and juices onto a platter. Serve with bread to mop up the juices.

Serves 4 as a starter

16 very large green (raw) prawns
2 teaspoons fennel seeds
2 teaspoons black peppercorns
2 teaspoons sea salt
4 cloves garlic, sliced
100 ml extra virgin olive oil
100 ml white wine or fino sherry
1 handful flat-leaf parsley leaves, chopped
strips of warmed Turkish bread, to serve

Fried calamari with fennel salt and saffron mayonnaise

This is my take on salt and pepper squid. The fennel salt adds an exotic flavour that works really well.

Grind the salt and fennel seeds in a coffee grinder or mortar and pestle.

Place the saffron and soaking liquid in a medium bowl, add the mayonnaise, salt, pepper and lemon juice and stir to combine.

Use a sharp knife to score the calamari, then cut into bite-sized pieces and halve the tentacles. Dust the calamari pieces with flour and shake off any excess.

Heat the cottonseed oil in a shallow frying pan over high heat. Add the calamari to the pan in batches and fry for about 3 minutes or until golden and just cooked. Drain on paper towels.

Sprinkle the fennel salt over the calamari to taste (serve the rest in a bowl on the side). Arrange the calamari on a bed of rocket leaves, and serve with the saffron mayonnaise and lemon wedges.

Serves 4

2 tablespoons sea salt
2 tablespoons fennel seeds
pinch of saffron threads soaked in 3 tablespoons
  boiling water
¾ cup good-quality mayonnaise
sea salt and freshly ground black pepper
½ lemon, juiced
700 g cleaned calamari with tentacles
200 g plain flour
800 ml cottonseed oil (see glossary)
rocket leaves, to serve
lemon wedges, to serve

Cannellini bean, calamari and chorizo salad

This recipe has a bit of a kick but you can adjust the chilli quantity or leave out the seeds to suit your taste. It works beautifully as part of a barbecue buffet, and I also love serving it as a weekend lunch.

Heat 3 tablespoons olive oil in a medium frying pan over medium heat. Add the onion, red chilli and half the garlic, then add the bay leaf, salt and pepper and cook for 4 minutes. Stir in the chorizo and cook for 6 minutes, then add the cannellini beans, tomatoes, tomato paste, vinegar and 100 ml water and simmer until the liquid is absorbed.

Roughly chop half the coriander and stir it into the bean mixture. Keep warm.

Heat a splash of the remaining olive oil in a large frying pan over high heat. Add the calamari and cook, stirring, for 2 minutes. Add the green chilli, remaining garlic, half the basil and a splash of vinegar and cook, stirring, for about 30 seconds.

Transfer the mixture to a large bowl. Stir in the green onion, parsley, remaining basil and coriander, remaining olive oil and half the lemon juice.

Spread the beans on a platter and top with the calamari mixture. Pour the remaining lemon juice over the calamari and serve immediately.

Serves 4–6

150 ml extra virgin olive oil

1 onion, chopped

1 red chilli, finely sliced

2 cloves garlic, finely sliced

1 bay leaf

sea salt and freshly ground black pepper

200 g hot chorizo sausage, sliced

600 g canned cannellini beans, drained

400 g can chopped tomatoes

2 tablespoons tomato paste

2½ tablespoons sherry vinegar, plus an extra splash

2 handfuls coriander leaves

350 g cleaned calamari with tentacles, cut into thin strips and tentacles cut in half

1 green chilli, seeded and finely sliced

2 handfuls basil leaves, torn

3 green onions, sliced diagonally

1 handful flat-leaf parsley leaves

1 lemon, juiced

Chicken stock

Chicken wings produce stock with a lovely rich flavour, and roasting the bones gives it a beautiful golden colour. You could also add very ripe tomatoes or mushroom trimmings.

Preheat the oven to 220°C. Season the whole chicken or wings with sea salt, then place on a baking tray and bake for 20–30 minutes or until golden brown.

Transfer the chicken to a large stockpot and cover with cold water. Bring to the boil over medium heat, skimming frequently. Add the vegetables and herbs and bring back to the boil. Skim again. Stir in the peppercorns and salt and simmer over low heat for 2 hours.

Strain, reserving the chicken flesh for soups or salads. The stock will keep in the fridge for 6 days or you can freeze it for up to 3 months.

Makes 4–5 litres

1 large free-range chicken or 1.5 kg chicken wings
sea salt
2 carrots, coarsely chopped
2 sticks celery, chopped
1 bulb garlic, unpeeled and halved
2 large brown onions, unpeeled and halved
4 sprigs thyme
2 bay leaves
½ bunch oregano
2 handfuls flat-leaf parsley sprigs
1 tablespoon black peppercorns
1 tablespoon salt

Coq au vin

The classic French combination of bacon, mushrooms and thyme turns chicken into a delicious crowd-pleaser. Slow-cooked to rich and tender perfection, it's just the thing for a winter or autumn table.

Preheat the oven to 180°C. Season the chicken pieces with salt and pepper.

Heat the olive oil and 2 tablespoons butter in a large flameproof dish with a lid over medium heat. Add the pancetta and cook for 2 minutes. Add the chicken pieces and brown on all sides. Remove the chicken and pancetta.

Place the shallots, garlic, bay leaves and thyme in the dish and cook, stirring, for 2 minutes. Add the tomato paste and stock and stir well. Return the chicken and pancetta to the dish and cover with the red wine. Simmer for 3 minutes, then cover with the lid, place in the oven and bake for 45–60 minutes or until the chicken is cooked and tender.

Place the dish over high heat on the stovetop and simmer, uncovered, for 5 minutes or until the juices are reduced by half. Stir in the remaining butter.

Place the bacon in a non-stick frying pan over medium–high heat. Add the mushrooms and a little extra butter, if necessary. Cook the mushrooms for 5 minutes or until just tender, then stir in the parsley. Serve the chicken and juices topped with the bacon and mushroom mixture, with boiled or mashed potatoes on the side.

Serves 4

1 large free-range chicken, cut into 8 pieces
sea salt and freshly ground black pepper
2 tablespoons olive oil
60 g unsalted butter
8 slices pancetta (see glossary), coarsely chopped
12 golden shallots, peeled and thickly sliced
12 cloves garlic, peeled and smashed
2 bay leaves
3 sprigs thyme
2 tablespoons tomato paste
500 ml chicken stock (see facing page)
500–625 ml red wine
4 thick rashers bacon, coarsely chopped
200 g button mushrooms, quartered
6 sprigs flat-leaf parsley, leaves chopped

Pot-roasted quail stuffed with
sage and rice (see page 138)

Pot-roasted quail stuffed with sage and rice

Here's something a little different (not to mention impressive) to cook at home. The pancetta and sage complement the sweetness of the grapes and chestnuts beautifully. Recipe pictured previous pages.

Place 300 ml stock and 300 ml water in a medium saucepan over medium heat. Add the rice and 100 g butter and bring to the boil. Reduce the heat to low and simmer, covered, for 10 minutes. Drain if necessary.

Heat 2 tablespoons olive oil in a frying pan over medium heat. Cook the onion and garlic for 2–3 minutes, without browning. Add the rice and half the chopped sage, season with salt and pepper and stir well. Spread on a plate to cool. Chop the remaining butter and dot the chunks through the rice mixture.

Preheat the oven to 210°C. Season the quails inside and stuff with the rice mixture. Close the cavities with small skewers or toothpicks and wrap in pancetta or prosciutto.

Heat the extra butter and remaining oil in a large frying pan over high heat and cook the quails for 2 minutes each side or until brown. Place in an ovenproof dish and squash and scatter the grapes over the quails. Add the chestnuts and remaining stock, then cover and bake for 30 minutes or until cooked. Remove the lid and return to the oven for 15 minutes to brown the quails.

Place the quails on serving plates. Pour the pan juices into a small saucepan, add the remaining sage leaves and check the seasoning. Reduce over high heat for about 3 minutes or until slightly thickened. Spoon the juices, grapes and chestnuts over the quails and serve with a green salad.

Serves 6

750–800 ml chicken stock (see page 134)
1 cup long-grain rice
200 g unsalted butter, plus 20 g extra
4 tablespoons olive oil
1 brown onion, finely chopped
4 cloves garlic, finely chopped
16 sage leaves, chopped
sea salt and freshly ground black pepper
6 jumbo quails, wing tips removed
6 thin slices pancetta (see glossary) or prosciutto
2 bunches Muscat grapes, stems removed
12 fresh chestnuts, boiled, peeled and coarsely crumbled

Pot au feu

Try serving this instead of a traditional Sunday roast. It looks stunning and always inspires oohs and aahs when I bring it out to the table.

To make the stuffing, place a non-stick frying pan over high heat. Add the chicken livers and sear for 30 seconds each side. Remove and slice. Add the butter, shallots and garlic to the pan and cook over medium heat for 2–3 minutes. Stir in the thyme leaves, parsley and 2 sprigs finely chopped rosemary leaves. Transfer the mixture to a medium bowl and add the livers. Add the ham, egg and breadcrumbs, season with salt and pepper and stir well.

Spoon the stuffing into the cavity of the chicken and secure with the remaining rosemary sprigs (stripped of leaves), or use metal skewers. Place the chicken in a very large saucepan or stockpot and add the stock. Pour in just enough cold water to cover. Add the potatoes and bring to the boil over very low heat, skimming the surface as necessary.

Add the carrots, celery, tomatoes, leek and fennel and simmer over low heat for 45 minutes. Stir in the broad beans and borlotti beans (if using) and simmer for 4–5 minutes or until the chicken is cooked through. Remove the chicken and vegetables, then cook the liquid over high heat until it is reduced and sufficient for four to five servings. Check the seasoning.

Serve the carved chicken, stuffing and vegetables in warm bowls with a little of the broth.

Serves 4–5

1.4 kg free-range chicken
1.5 litres chicken stock (see page 134)
4 kipfler potatoes, halved
1 bunch Dutch (baby) carrots, scrubbed and trimmed
2 hearts celery, halved
1 punnet (250 g) cherry tomatoes
2 leeks, trimmed and cut into 4 cm pieces
1 bulb fennel, trimmed and cut into 8 wedges
½ cup podded fresh broad beans, blanched in boiling water and peeled
½ cup fresh borlotti beans (optional), simmered in water for 20 minutes

Herb stuffing

90 g organic chicken livers, trimmed and soaked in milk for 30 minutes, then drained and dried
50 g unsalted butter
6 golden shallots, chopped
4 cloves garlic, finely chopped
2 sprigs thyme, leaves only
½ bunch flat-leaf parsley, leaves chopped
6 long sprigs rosemary
90 g leg ham, chopped
1 free-range egg, lightly beaten
2 slices sourdough bread, crumbed in a food processor
sea salt and freshly ground black pepper

Marinated chicken with cinnamon, garlic and rosewater

The aromatic marinade pleases the senses, while the tart pomegranate dressing brings your palate to life.

Place the garlic, cinnamon, lemon juice, thyme leaves, pepper and salt to taste in a mortar and pestle and crush to a paste. Transfer to a large bowl, add the olive oil and rosewater and mix well. Massage the marinade into the chicken, then cover with plastic film and place in the fridge for 2 hours.

Preheat a chargrill or barbecue plate to medium–high. When hot, cook the chicken, turning regularly, for 20–25 minutes or until charred and cooked through. (Alternatively, heat 1 tablespoon olive oil in a frying pan over high heat and sear the chicken, skin-side down, for about 2 minutes, then roast in a 200°C oven for 20–25 minutes or until cooked through.)

To make the dressing, place all the ingredients in a bowl and stir to combine.

To serve, pour the dressing over the hot chicken and scatter with almonds, mint and watercress sprigs. Garnish with rose petals, if using, and serve with spinach, rice and yoghurt salad with almonds (see page 55).

Serves 2

3 cloves garlic
1½ teaspoons ground cinnamon
½ lemon, juiced
4 sprigs thyme, leaves only
1 teaspoon freshly ground black pepper
sea salt
4 tablespoons olive oil
120 ml rosewater
1.2 kg free-range chicken, cut in half
3 tablespoons toasted almonds
mint leaves and watercress sprigs, to serve
rose petals, to garnish (optional)

Dressing

1½ small red chillies, finely sliced
3 tablespoons pomegranate molasses (see glossary)
½ teaspoon ground cinnamon
½ clove garlic, finely chopped
1 tablespoon rosewater
4 tablespoons olive oil
1 teaspoon castor sugar

Quail saltimbocca with pears and sherry vinegar

The texture and fruitiness of the pears and the saltiness of the prosciutto combine to give quail a delicious makeover. This is a fabulous starter.

Melt the butter in a large frying pan over medium heat. Add the pears and sugar, season with salt and pepper and toss gently. Stir in the vinegar and cook until it evaporates. Remove from the heat and keep warm.

Wrap each quail in a slice of prosciutto, then secure a sage leaf on top with a toothpick. Heat a large frying pan over high heat and add the olive oil. Cook the quails, breast-side down, for 5–6 minutes or until browned. Turn them over, add the white wine and cook for a further 5–6 minutes or until cooked to your liking. Add the pears and return to the boil, then remove from the heat and allow the quails to rest for 3–4 minutes.

Arrange the rocket on a large platter and sit the quails and pears on top. Remove the toothpicks and drizzle with the pan juices before serving.

Serves 4 as a starter

40 g unsalted butter
2 beurre bosc pears, peeled, cored and each cut
  into 8 pieces
60 g brown sugar
sea salt and freshly ground black pepper
2½ tablespoons sherry vinegar
4 jumbo quails, boned and butterflied
  (ask your butcher to do this)
4 slices prosciutto
4 large sage leaves
4 tablespoons extra virgin olive oil
3 tablespoons white wine
1 bunch rocket leaves

Chicken with peas and braised cos lettuce

This is possibly the best braised chicken ever, and is fabulous as is. If you're after a more substantial meal, serve it with mashed potato.

Rub the chicken halves with the garlic paste and thyme leaves, then season with salt and pepper.

Heat the olive oil in a large frying pan over medium heat, add the chicken, skin-side down, and brown for 4–5 minutes. Turn the chicken and add the lettuce and half the butter. Brown the lettuce on both sides, then remove it from the pan. Stir in the vinegar, then add the stock and turn the chicken over. Cover, bring to the boil, then simmer over medium heat for about 20–25 minutes or until the chicken is cooked.

Return the lettuce to the pan and simmer, uncovered, for 3 minutes. Stir in the peas and remaining butter, then remove the chicken and lettuce. Cook the sauce over high heat until reduced and glossy. Serve the chicken, lettuce and peas with the sauce spooned over the top.

Serves 2

1.2 kg free-range chicken, halved and with neck, backbone and thigh bones removed (ask your butcher to do this)
2 cloves garlic, mashed with 1 teaspoon extra virgin olive oil in a mortar and pestle
4 sprigs thyme, leaves only
sea salt and freshly ground black pepper
100 ml extra virgin olive oil
1 baby cos lettuce, halved
100 g unsalted butter
1½ tablespoons sherry vinegar
400 ml chicken stock (see page 134)
1 cup frozen baby peas

Chicken fricassee with sherry vinegar, tomato, paprika and broad beans

Smoked paprika can easily overpower a dish but it's just delicious when used correctly. It works particularly well with the sherry vinegar.

Rub the paprika, salt and pepper all over the chicken pieces.

Heat the olive oil in a large heavy-based frying pan over medium heat. Add the chicken and brown on all sides. Add the garlic, shallots and bay leaf and cook for 5 minutes. Stir in the tomato paste and vinegar and bring to the boil. Add the stock, then cover and cook over low heat for 10–15 minutes.

Remove the lid and cook over high heat for 5–7 minutes or until the sauce is reduced and the chicken is almost cooked. Add the broad beans and cook for 4–5 minutes or until the chicken is cooked through. Stir in the butter. Serve with steamed rice or mashed potato.

Serves 4

1 teaspoon smoked paprika
1 teaspoon sweet paprika
sea salt and freshly ground black pepper
1.2 kg free-range chicken, cut into 8 pieces
2 tablespoons olive oil
4 cloves garlic, finely sliced
6 red shallots, sliced
1 bay leaf
2 tablespoons tomato paste
100 ml sherry vinegar
400 ml chicken stock (see page 134)
1 cup podded fresh broad beans, blanched in boiling water and peeled
knob of unsalted butter
steamed rice or mashed potato, to serve

Pot-roasted chicken with lemon and garlic

The slow-roasted garlic turns into a nutty, buttery paste and flavours the chicken perfectly. This is delicious served with buttered Brussels sprouts and peas. Recipe pictured following pages.

Preheat the oven to 165°C. Use a knife to trim the fat from the chicken cavity, then dry the chicken inside and out with paper towels.

Combine the salt, fennel seeds and pepper. Rub the chicken inside and out with the salt mixture, then place a few lemon slices inside the chicken. Transfer the chicken to a heavy-based ovenproof dish. Push some of the butter and thyme under the skin, then place the rest inside the chicken. Add the garlic, potatoes and remaining lemon slices to the dish.

Pour olive oil over the chicken. Add the bay leaf and wine to the dish and put the lid on. Make a flour paste by combining the flour and water, adjusting the quantities if necessary – the dough should be sticky but able to be handled. Seal the dish with the paste and bake for 1 hour.

Serves 4–6

1.6 kg free-range chicken
3 tablespoons sea salt
1½ teaspoons ground fennel seeds
1½ teaspoons freshly ground black pepper
2 large lemons, sliced into 5 mm thick rounds
60 g unsalted butter
5 sprigs thyme
2 bulbs garlic, unpeeled, lightly crushed
6 small potatoes (spunta or kipfler), unpeeled, sliced into rounds
100 ml olive oil
1 bay leaf
200 ml white wine
220 g plain flour
150 ml water

Pot-roasted chicken with lemon and garlic (see page 145)

Roasted guinea fowl with mandarin and juniper berries, grape salad and parsnip chips

This recipe is the result of the first time I cooked guinea fowl at home. Instead of fussing with jus and stock, I decided to make a warm autumn salad, giving maximum focus to the flavours.

Preheat the oven to 220°C. Season the breast and legs of the guinea fowl. Combine the crushed juniper berries and thyme with some of the butter and slide under the skin of the breast. Lay the pancetta slices over the legs and breast.

Heat a cast-iron casserole dish over high heat and quickly brown the legs and breast, skin-side down. Add the mandarin zest then, with the skin-side facing up, put the dish in the oven and roast for 14 minutes. Remove from the oven and add the juice from the mandarin and a splash of verjuice. Rest for 10 minutes before carving.

Meanwhile, to make the salad, combine the grapes, onion and parsley in a bowl. Drizzle with a little olive oil, season and toss to combine.

To make the chips, gently fry the parsnip ribbons in olive oil until golden. Drain on paper towel and season well.

Remove the bird from the dish and slice the breast and leg meat. Put the dish over medium heat, add the rest of the butter and warm through. Season to taste.

Arrange the salad on individual plates, place the guinea fowl on top and spoon on the warmed juices. Serve with parsnip chips on the side.

Serves 2

1.2 kg guinea fowl, legs separated from the breast
sea salt and freshly ground black pepper
2 teaspoons crushed juniper berries
4 sprigs thyme, leaves only
80 g butter
4 thin slices pancetta (see glossary)
1 mandarin, zest removed with a vegetable peeler, then juiced
verjuice (see glossary), to taste

Parsnip chips

1 parsnip, cut into thick ribbons with a vegetable peeler
olive oil, for shallow-frying

Grape salad

1 small bunch black grapes, seeded and sliced
½ small red onion, sliced into half-moons
2 handfuls flat-leaf parsley leaves, torn
extra virgin olive oil
sea salt and freshly ground black pepper

Syrian chicken with ginger, lemon and saffron

While I was on holiday recently a patch of cooler weather called for hearty fare, and this chicken braise was the result. It has since proved to be a real favourite – the heady but gentle spice mix is just perfect for chicken. This must-try dish can easily be doubled to feed the masses.

Combine the salt, cumin, cinnamon, pepper and turmeric in a large plastic bag. Add the chicken pieces and shake to coat.

Heat the olive oil in a large heavy-based saucepan over high heat. Add the chicken and brown on all sides. Remove from the pan and set aside. Add the onion, ginger, garlic and chilli to the pan and cook for 3 minutes, adding a little more oil if necessary. Add the tomato, saffron threads, cumin seeds and thyme and cook for 2 minutes.

Return the chicken to the pan and add the lemon juice and zest, honey, currants, stock powder and enough water to just cover the chicken. Cover with a lid and simmer over medium heat for 10 minutes. Uncover and simmer for 10–15 minutes or until the chicken is tender and cooked through, and the sauce is slightly reduced. Stir in the coriander and serve with couscous or rice.

Serves 4

2 teaspoons sea salt
2 teaspoons ground cumin
2 teaspoons ground cinnamon
1 teaspoon freshly ground black pepper
1 teaspoon ground turmeric
1.4–1.6 kg free-range chicken, cut into 8 pieces
100 ml olive oil
2 brown onions, thickly sliced
100 g fresh ginger, cut into matchsticks
5 cloves garlic, peeled and smashed
2 small red chillies, split
2 tomatoes, coarsely chopped
2 pinches of saffron threads
½ teaspoon cumin seeds
5 sprigs thyme, leaves only
coarsely grated zest and juice of 1 lemon
2 tablespoons honey
100 g currants
2 tablespoons vegetable stock powder
½ bunch coriander, leaves only

Turkey with pistachio, thyme and cumin stuffing and cranberry and orange glaze

This elaborate Christmas dinner will make any tasteless, dry turkey you've had to endure in the past pale into insignificance. It is worth sourcing an organic turkey – the flavour will be far superior.

To make the stuffing, heat the olive oil in a medium frying pan over low heat. Cook the shallots and garlic for 5 minutes or until soft. Add the pancetta and cook for 6 minutes. Stir in the cumin, coriander and baharat, then remove from the heat. Squeeze the bread and crumble into a large bowl. Add the salt, pepper, preserved lemon or pickled orange, thyme, coriander, parsley, eggs, pistachios, butter and shallot mixture. Stir to combine and check the seasoning.

Preheat the oven to 240°C. Season the turkey and spoon the stuffing into the cavity. Tie the legs and tail together and secure tightly. Layer the pancetta over the breast and legs. Place the onion slices in a baking tray and sit the turkey on top (it should fit snugly). Pour in the stock and water and cover with a large sheet of baking paper. Seal with foil and bake for 1¾ hours.

Reduce the oven temperature to 190°C. Uncover the turkey, baste well with the juices and bake for a further 1½ hours or until browned and cooked (cover loosely with foil to prevent over-browning if necessary). Set aside for 20 minutes before carving.

Meanwhile, toss the carrots and asparagus in olive oil in a small baking tray. Season and bake for the last hour of the turkey cooking time.

To make the glaze, drain most of the turkey juices into a small saucepan. Add the cranberries and orange juice and boil over high heat until reduced to the desired consistency. Check the seasoning.

To serve, place the turkey on a platter, surround with the vegetables and spoon a little glaze over the top. Serve the remaining glaze on the side.

Serves 8–12

5 kg organic turkey, cavity and wing tips trimmed and dried inside and out
150 g pancetta (see glossary), sliced
2 brown onions, unpeeled and thickly sliced
800 ml chicken stock (see page 134)
250 ml water
3 bunches Dutch (baby) carrots, peeled
3 bunches white asparagus, trimmed
125 ml extra virgin olive oil
1 cup dried cranberries, simmered in the juice of 2 oranges for 8 minutes

Stuffing

125 ml extra virgin olive oil
8 golden shallots, sliced
6 cloves garlic, finely sliced
150 g pancetta (see glossary), sliced
3 teaspoons ground cumin
3 teaspoons ground coriander
3 teaspoons baharat (see glossary)
6 thick slices sourdough bread, crusts removed and soaked in milk for 15 minutes
sea salt and freshly ground black pepper
3 tablespoons finely chopped preserved lemon or pickled orange rind
½ bunch thyme, leaves chopped
5 sprigs coriander, chopped
5 sprigs flat-leaf parsley, chopped
2 free-range eggs
1 cup pistachio kernels, chopped
250 g unsalted butter, chopped

Noodle soup with chicken balls and corn

This soup appeals to little and big kids alike – and it's a great way to warm up from the inside out.

Place the chicken (without breasts), onion, garlic, celery, carrot, herbs, peppercorns and salt in a large stockpot. Cover with cold water and bring to the boil over high heat. Reduce the heat to low and simmer, partially covered, for 1 hour.

Coarsely chop the chicken breasts and place in a food processor with the parmesan and 1 egg. Season to taste and process until smooth. Chill the mixture in the fridge for 20–30 minutes, then roll into walnut-sized balls.

Strain the chicken stock, return the liquid to the pot and set the chicken carcass aside. When cool, remove the leg meat and shred it. Bring the stock to a simmer over medium heat, skimming the top if necessary. Add the spaghetti and simmer for 5 minutes. Add the corn, chicken balls and leg meat and simmer for 5–6 minutes. Whisk the remaining eggs and add to the soup with the lemon juice. Return to a simmer, check the seasoning and drizzle with olive oil to serve.

Serves 6–8

1.2–1.4 kg free-range chicken, breasts removed
2 brown onions, unpeeled and halved
1 bulb garlic, unpeeled and halved
2 sticks celery, coarsely chopped
1 carrot, coarsely chopped
10 sprigs flat-leaf parsley
2 bay leaves
3 sprigs thyme
1 tablespoon black peppercorns
2 teaspoons sea salt
30 g grated parmesan
3 free-range eggs
sea salt and freshly ground black pepper
200 g spaghetti, broken into 6 cm pieces
3 corn cobs, boiled for 5 minutes and kernels
   removed
½ lemon, juiced
2½ tablespoons olive oil

Chargrilled quail with rocket and grape salad

Vine leaves help keep the quail moist, the sweetness of the saba (also called vincotto) pairs well with the slightly gamy flavours, and the sharpness of the goat's cheese sneaks in for a bit of contrast.

Combine the verjuice and olive oil in a small bowl. Place the quail in a shallow dish, then pour on half the verjuice mixture, turning the quail to coat. Add the thyme and garlic and toss gently. Set aside for 40 minutes.

Preheat a barbecue or chargrill to medium. Place a folded vine leaf on each quail, then fold the quail in half to enclose the vine leaf and secure with a bamboo skewer. Barbecue the quails for 4–5 minutes on one side, drizzling with the marinade, then turn and cook for a further 4–5 minutes or until cooked as desired.

Combine the grapes, rocket and remaining verjuice mixture in a bowl and place half on the serving plates or platter. Top with the quail and goat's cheese, then add the remaining grape mixture. Drizzle with saba and serve.

Serves 4 as a starter

100 ml verjuice (see glossary)
100 ml extra virgin olive oil
4 quails, semi-boned, drumstick and winglet attached
6 sprigs thyme, leaves only
2 cloves garlic, chopped
4 large vine leaves (from specialty food shops)
4 bamboo skewers, soaked in cold water
   for 20 minutes
200 g seedless green grapes, sliced into rounds
1 large bunch rocket, trimmed
4 tablespoons soft goat's cheese
100 ml saba (see glossary)

Chicken and vegetable brodo

With rice and pasta, this soup is a complete meal in a bowl, which is just the thing for cold, wet weather. It will keep in the fridge for a week and freeze for two months. Garlic bruschetta is delicious with hearty soups: simply toast slices of crusty bread, then brush with olive oil and rub with garlic.

Preheat the oven to 220°C. Toss the chicken wings in 1 tablespoon olive oil and season with salt and pepper. Place on a baking tray and bake for 25–30 minutes or until golden brown.

Place the wings in a large stockpot and cover with the stock and water. Bring to the boil over medium heat, then simmer for 15–20 minutes or until very tender. Strain (reserving the stock) and set aside. Leave to cool slightly, then remove the meat and about half the skin.

Heat 2 tablespoons olive oil in the stockpot over medium heat. Cook the onion, garlic, oregano, thyme and bay leaf for 2–3 minutes, then add the fennel, carrots and celery and cook for a further 10 minutes. Add the chicken meat and skin, reserved stock, rice and spaghetti and bring to the boil over high heat. Reduce the heat to medium and simmer for 5–8 minutes. Stir in the zucchini, peas and parsley and simmer for a further 5 minutes or until the rice and pasta are cooked. Add the remaining olive oil and serve with bruschetta and grated parmesan, if using.

Serves 10

1 kg chicken wings
4 tablespoons olive oil
sea salt and freshly ground black pepper
2 litres chicken stock (see page 134)
1 litre water
2 onions, chopped
4 cloves garlic, chopped
4 sprigs oregano
4 sprigs thyme
1 bay leaf
1 bulb fennel, trimmed and chopped
2 carrots, sliced
½ bunch celery, chopped
½ cup arborio rice
50 g spaghetti, broken into 6 cm pieces
2 zucchini (courgettes), chopped
½ cup frozen peas
½ bunch flat-leaf parsley, leaves chopped
crusty bread or garlic bruschetta, to serve
grated parmesan, to serve (optional)

Chicken livers with sumac, currants and radicchio

The combination of rich livers, sweet currants, bitter radicchio and tart lemon dressing delights the palate from every angle. This dish will win over just about anyone, even those who don't usually like liver.

Combine the lemon juice, vinegar, onion, sumac, currants, radicchio, parsley, croutons and half the olive oil in a large bowl. Stir well.

Heat a large non-stick frying pan over high heat. Add the remaining olive oil and the chicken livers. Season and cook for 1 minute, then turn, add the oregano and butter and cook for a further minute. Add extra lemon juice, if desired, and pour the liver mixture over the salad. Toss to combine and serve immediately.

Serves 4 as a starter

1 lemon, juiced
1 tablespoon red wine vinegar
1 small red onion, halved and sliced lengthways
3–4 tablespoons sumac (see glossary)
3 tablespoons currants, covered with red wine vinegar
  and brought to the boil, then drained
1 heart radicchio, shredded
1 handful flat-leaf parsley, leaves only
3 slices toasted rye bread, rubbed with garlic
  and cut into croutons
125 ml extra virgin olive oil
400 g fresh organic chicken livers, trimmed, soaked
  in milk for 30 minutes, then drained
sea salt and freshly ground black pepper
handful oregano leaves
2 knobs of unsalted butter
lemon juice, extra (optional)

Black pepper, walnut and cumin-stuffed chicken roasted with pumpkin

This divine spiced chicken with unexpected walnut stuffing works perfectly with the pumpkin, and do make the grape, burghul and witlof salad (see page 67) to go with it.

Preheat the oven to 220°C.

Heat half the oil in a medium frying pan over medium heat and cook the walnuts and garlic, tossing, for 3 minutes. Add the cumin seeds and season with a little salt. Cook for another 2 minutes, then pour the mixture into a mortar and pestle. Add the peppercorns, thyme and remaining salt and pound to a rough paste.

Gently separate the skin from the flesh in pockets all over the chicken and stuff with the paste, adding small cubes of butter as you go.

Spread out the pumpkin wedges in a baking dish, season with salt and pepper and drizzle with the remaining oil. Sit the chicken on top and roast for 45–55 minutes until cooked and golden brown. Rest for about 10 minutes before carving.

Serves 4

100 ml extra virgin olive oil
¾ cup walnuts
4 cloves garlic, split
3 teaspoons cumin seeds
3 tablespoons sea salt flakes
2 teaspoons black peppercorns
6 sprigs thyme, leaves only
1.4 kg free-range organic chicken, butterflied
  (ask your butcher to do this)
100 g butter, cut into small cubes
1 jap pumpkin, skin on, cut into 8 wedges
sea salt and freshly ground black pepper

Baked corned beef

An oldie but a goodie – I can't go past this classic example of comfort food. It's also delicious served with spring cabbage cooked in apple cider.

Preheat the oven to 180°C. Place the beef in a large ovenproof dish and cover with cold water. Bring to the boil over high heat, then remove the beef and drain the liquid. Return the beef to the dish, add the bay leaves, peppercorns, carrots, celery, leeks, parsley, garlic and thyme and cover with boiling water. Bring to a simmer over medium heat, then cover and cook in the oven for 2½ hours or until tender.

Meanwhile, to make the mustard kipflers, boil the potatoes in lightly salted water for about 15–20 minutes or until tender. Drain and place in a large bowl. Add the onion, cream and mustards, then season. Toss gently to combine.

Remove the beef from the dish and discard the other flavourings. Cut the beef into slices and serve with the mustard kipfler potatoes and watercress sprigs.

Serves 6

1.5 kg piece corned beef
2 bay leaves
2 tablespoons black peppercorns
2 carrots, sliced
3 sticks celery, sliced
2 leeks, trimmed and sliced
¼ bunch flat-leaf parsley
1 whole bulb garlic, unpeeled, cut in half
   lengthways and cloves separated
4 sprigs thyme
watercress sprigs, to serve

Mustard kipflers
8 large kipfler potatoes, sliced
1 red onion, sliced
200 ml pouring cream
4 tablespoons Dijon mustard
3 tablespoons seeded mustard
sea salt and freshly ground black pepper

> Steak tartare

This simple, light dish of raw beef should be quite spicy and served just below room temperature to be at its best. I like to use soft-boiled eggs instead of the traditional raw egg in the dressing.

Combine the beef, garlic, shallots, mustard, horseradish, capers, Tabasco, Worcestershire sauce, salt and half the olive oil in a large bowl. Stir gently and add the parsley and lemon juice, then stir again.

In a separate bowl, combine the celery leaves and watercress sprigs with the remaining olive oil and toss.

Spread the beef mixture on a serving plate, scatter with the salad leaves and break the eggs over the top. Sprinkle with pepper and extra horseradish and serve with toasted baguette.

Serves 6 as a starter

400 g beef eye fillet, finely chopped
1 small clove garlic, very finely chopped
3 large golden shallots, finely chopped
2 tablespoons Dijon mustard
3 tablespoons grated fresh horseradish,
   plus extra to serve
3 tablespoons capers, drained
4–6 drops of Tabasco sauce
3 teaspoons Worcestershire sauce
sea salt, to taste
100 ml extra virgin olive oil
6 sprigs parsley, leaves chopped
1–2 tablespoons lemon juice
10 celery leaves
1 bunch watercress, broken into small sprigs
2 free-range eggs, boiled for 7 minutes and peeled
freshly ground black pepper
thinly sliced baguette, toasted, to serve

< Beef short ribs in fragrant Thai sauce

These ribs have a wonderfully intense flavour. They are so easy to make, and there's practically no mess to clean up – a perfect do-ahead dish for dinner with friends.

Preheat the oven to 150°C. Heat the oil in a wok or frying pan over medium heat and brown the ribs for 3–4 minutes on each side. Remove from the pan. Add the onion and cook for 2 minutes or until soft and golden.

Place the ribs, onion, galangal, lemongrass, ginger, fish sauce, palm sugar, garlic, stock, water, lime leaves, tamarind and chillies in a very large ovenproof dish. Stir to combine and bring to a simmer over medium heat. Cover and bake in the oven for at least 2 hours (remove the lid for the last 10 minutes) or until the ribs are very tender.

Sprinkle the ribs with coriander, basil and chilli, if using, and serve with lime cheeks and steamed rice.

Serves 4

2½ tablespoons vegetable oil
8 short beef ribs (about 180 g each)
2 brown onions, sliced
4 cm piece galangal, sliced
4 cm piece lemongrass, very finely sliced
4 cm piece fresh ginger, sliced
130 ml fish sauce
130 g palm sugar
3 cloves garlic, bruised
500 ml chicken stock (see page 134)
1 litre water
2 kaffir lime leaves
4 tablespoons tamarind puree
5 small red or green chillies
½ bunch coriander leaves (optional)
½ bunch Thai basil leaves, torn (optional)
1 large green chilli, sliced (optional)
2 limes, cut into cheeks

Eye fillet steak with horseradish cream

Good-quality steak needs little embellishment, but the peppery flavour of fresh horseradish with beef is a match made in heaven.

Combine the horseradish and crème fraîche in a bowl and stir well.

Brush both sides of the steaks with half the oil and season well with salt and pepper. Heat a large non-stick frying pan over high heat and when hot, cook the steaks for 5 minutes on one side. Turn, add more oil if necessary, and cook for a further 3–4 minutes for rare, or until cooked to your liking.

Toss the radishes and watercress in a bowl with a little oil.

Slice the steaks in half, place on serving plates and top with a dollop of horseradish cream. Drizzle with a little olive oil and serve with the radish salad and some boiled potatoes.

Serves 4

1–2 tablespoons grated fresh horseradish
120 g crème fraîche or light sour cream
4 eye fillet steaks (about 180 g each)
150 ml extra virgin olive oil
sea salt and freshly ground black pepper
6 red radishes, sliced
½ bunch watercress, broken into sprigs

Pickled veal tongue with salsa verde and boiled potatoes

Don't be put off – cooked this way, tongue tastes like the best corned beef ever and is delicious with salsa verde. You will need to order it from your butcher in advance.

Place the tongue in a large saucepan and cover with cold water. Add the garlic, bay leaf and peppercorns, then cook, covered, over low heat for about 2 hours or until tender. Remove the tongue and discard the seasonings. Allow to cool slightly, then remove the tongue's outer skin, wrap the meat in plastic film and chill.

For the salsa verde, combine all the ingredients, plus black pepper to taste, in a blender or food processor and process until smooth.

Cook the potatoes in boiling water over medium heat for 5 minutes or until tender. Drain, season with salt and pepper and toss with the olive oil, mustard and vinegar.

Slice the tongue into 1 cm thick slices. Heat the extra oil in a frying pan over medium heat and cook the slices for 2 minutes each side or until browned.

Divide the potato and watercress among serving plates, top with the tongue slices and half an egg. Spoon on the salsa verde and serve.

Serves 6

1 pickled yearling beef tongue
1 bulb garlic
1 bay leaf
10 peppercorns
4 desiree potatoes, cut into 1 cm slices
sea salt and freshly ground black pepper
2½ tablespoons extra virgin olive oil,
   plus extra for shallow-frying
2 tablespoons Dijon mustard
2½ tablespoons red wine vinegar
watercress sprigs, to serve
3 free-range eggs, soft-boiled and peeled

Salsa verde
3 handfuls flat-leaf parsley leaves
3 tablespoons capers
2 gherkins
5 green olives, pitted
1 clove garlic
2 handfuls oregano leaves
125 ml extra virgin olive oil
1 anchovy

Scotch fillet steak with herb butter and onion fritters

The tastiest cut of beef for a simple steak is scotch fillet. And it's well worth making the onion fritters – they're sensational.

For the onion fritters, separate the onion rings and place in a bowl. Cover with milk and set aside for at least 1 hour. Add the egg yolk and stir. Drain the onion rings and dust in flour, shaking off any excess. Heat the oil in a large frying pan (at least 6 cm deep) and, when hot (180°C), deep-fry the onion rings until golden. Drain on paper towels and keep warm until ready to serve.

To make the herb butter, combine the butter, fennel, pepper, mustard, horseradish and olive oil in a food processor and process briefly. Add the garlic and shallots and process until combined. Add the herbs and pulse briefly, then transfer the mixture to a bowl.

Heat a chargrill or barbecue plate until hot. Season the steaks with salt and pepper on one side and cook, seasoned-side down, for 4 minutes. Turn and cook for another 1–2 minutes for rare, or until cooked as desired. Top the steaks with a large dollop of herb butter. Roll the remaining herb butter in baking paper, then in foil and place in the freezer until needed.

Combine the watercress or rocket with the lemon juice. Serve the steaks with onion fritters and watercress or rocket.

Serves 4

4 scotch fillet steaks (about 250 g each)
sea salt and freshly ground black pepper
1 bunch watercress or rocket
1 tablespoon lemon juice

Herb butter

125 g unsalted butter, softened
2 teaspoons ground fennel
2 teaspoons freshly ground black pepper
2 teaspoons Dijon mustard
1 tablespoon grated horseradish
1½ tablespoons olive oil
2 small cloves garlic, chopped
3 golden shallots, chopped
¼ bunch parsley, leaves only
¼ bunch chervil, leaves only
¼ bunch chives, snipped

Onion fritters

2 brown onions, cut into thick rings
200 ml milk
1 free-range egg yolk
¾ cup plain flour
vegetable oil, for frying

Martini family stuffed capsicums

My mum learned to make these stuffed capsicums from her mother-in-law and they were my family's version of meat and three veg. For a complete meal, serve them with rice, couscous or mashed potato.

Preheat the oven to 200°C. Trim the tops off the capsicums and remove the seeds.

Heat half the olive oil in a large frying pan over medium heat and cook the onion and garlic for 2 minutes. Add the cinnamon, chilli and mint, then season with salt and pepper and remove from the heat.

Place the mince, eggs, breadcrumbs, onion mixture and parsley in a food processor and process until well combined (you may need to do this in batches).

Spoon the mixture into the capsicums. Place the remaining oil in an ovenproof dish, add the capsicums and bake for 10–15 minutes or until lightly browned. Pour the tomato passata and chopped tomatoes over the capsicums and add the peas and 1 cup water. Cover and bake for a further 40 minutes.

Serves 6

6 large red or green capsicums (peppers)
100 ml extra virgin olive oil
2 brown onions, finely chopped
6 cloves garlic, finely chopped
3 teaspoons ground cinnamon
2 teaspoons dried chilli
3 teaspoons dried mint
sea salt and freshly ground black pepper
1 kg beef mince
2 large free-range eggs
1½ cups freshly made breadcrumbs
½ bunch flat-leaf parsley, leaves coarsely chopped
4 cups tomato passata
400 g can chopped tomatoes
1 cup frozen peas

Beef kofta on skewers with lemon

Hand these skewers around with a squeeze of lemon juice. They go beautifully with spinach, rice and yoghurt salad with almonds (see page 55).

Place the beef in a food processor and process for 30 seconds. Add the remaining ingredients, except the olive oil and lemon wedges, and process for 2 minutes. Add 3–4 tablespoons cold water and process to a paste.

Divide the mixture into 10 portions, and mould each around a skewer. Brush with olive oil and refrigerate until firm.

Cook on a hot barbecue for 6–8 minutes or until cooked to your liking. Serve with lemon wedges.

Makes 10

500 g lean scotch fillet, diced
1 red onion, chopped
3 cloves garlic, chopped
2½ teaspoons ground cumin
2½ teaspoons dried mint
1 teaspoon dried chilli flakes
1 teaspoon sea salt
freshly ground black pepper
olive oil, for brushing
lemon wedges, to serve

Bistecchina with ricotta and balsamic dressing

You'll be surprised at just how well fresh ricotta works with bistecchina, which is thinly sliced steak.

Preheat the oven to 220°C. Place the capsicums on a lightly greased oven tray and roast for 15 minutes, turning once. Remove and place in a plastic bag for 15 minutes. Remove the skins and seeds and chop coarsely.

Transfer the capsicum pieces to a bowl and season with salt and pepper. Add the garlic, basil, parsley and 1 tablespoon olive oil, stir to combine and set aside.

Heat a large oiled frying pan over high heat. Season the steaks, drizzle with 1½ tablespoons olive oil and cook, one at a time, for 30 seconds on each side or until cooked to your liking.

Place the steaks on serving plates and top with the capsicum mixture and a dollop of ricotta. Toss the rocket leaves with balsamic vinegar and the remaining olive oil and scatter over the steaks. Serve with lemon wedges.

Serves 4

6 banana capsicums (see glossary)
sea salt and freshly ground black pepper
1 clove garlic, finely chopped
1 cup basil leaves, torn
1 cup flat-leaf parsley leaves, torn
100 ml extra virgin olive oil
4 × 175 g pieces scotch fillet, flattened
200 g ricotta
1 large bunch rocket, trimmed
2½ tablespoons balsamic vinegar
lemon wedges, to serve

Roast rump of beef

This cut of meat is often overlooked for roasting but the results are utterly delicious. Rump has a better depth of flavour than fillet and a good covering of fat. A great roast to serve when you are having people over for dinner.

Preheat the oven to 220°C. Use a sharp knife to score the beef fat, then push the rosemary sprigs and slivers of garlic into the cuts. Season the beef and brush with some of the olive oil, then sear in a frying pan for about 5 minutes or until golden. Transfer to a roasting tin.

Brush the carrots and shallots with the remaining olive oil. Place the carrots, shallots and potatoes around the beef and roast for 50–60 minutes or until cooked to your liking, turning the vegetables once. Rest the beef, covered, in a warm place for at least 15 minutes before carving.

To make the sauce, place all the ingredients in a food processor and process until smooth.

Serve the beef and vegetables in the roasting tin with the pan juices, and the horseradish and bread sauce on the side.

Serves 8

1.8 kg piece aged beef rump with fat
4 sprigs rosemary
1 bulb garlic, cloves peeled and sliced
sea salt and freshly ground black pepper
4 tablespoons olive oil
4 carrots, halved lengthways
10 golden shallots, unpeeled, halved
8 small potatoes, parboiled for 15 minutes, drained,
   then tossed in a saucepan to roughen the edges

Horseradish and bread sauce
150 g fresh horseradish, grated (or you can use
   store-bought pre-grated horseradish)
3 slices white bread, torn into pieces
2 teaspoons hot English mustard
100 ml olive oil
100 ml pouring cream
sea salt
100 ml water

Braised honey, soy and ginger spare ribs

This rich, unctuous braise needs little effort. The ribs have so much meat on them you need only one per person.

Preheat the oven to 170°C.

Place all the ingredients in a large ovenproof dish, stir and bring to a simmer over medium heat. Transfer to the oven and bake, covered, for 1½ hours. Remove the lid, increase the oven temperature to 200°C and bake for a further 5–8 minutes or until the ribs are browned.

Remove the ribs, skim the fat from the juices and reduce over high heat until syrupy.

Serve the ribs on a platter with some of the juices drizzled over the top. Scatter with coriander leaves and serve with steamed or fried rice (see page 80).

Serves 6

6 pork spare ribs
1 brown onion, sliced
4 tablespoons light soy sauce
100 ml oyster sauce
250 ml Chinese rice wine
250 ml water
4 cm piece fresh ginger, finely sliced
4 cloves garlic, smashed
1 cinnamon stick
1½ teaspoons Chinese five-spice powder
4 tablespoons honey
1 red chilli, split
1 teaspoon dried chilli flakes
coriander leaves, to serve

> Braised organic bacon with dried cherries and peaches

This dish is rich and intense as the long marinating time allows the flavours to really penetrate the cured meat. It's a great alternative to the classic Sunday roast, but do make sure you buy a piece of quality organic bacon.

Combine all the ingredients except the peaches in a large bowl. Cover and place in the fridge for 3–5 hours, turning the bacon occasionally.

Preheat the oven to 220°C. Place the bacon in a baking dish, cover with foil and cook for 45 minutes. Add the peaches, baste well with the juices and cook, covered, for 15–20 minutes or until the bacon is cooked.

Remove the bacon and peaches from the baking dish. Place the dish over high heat and simmer until the sauce has reduced, if desired.

Cut the bacon into thick slices with the rind on. Arrange on plates with the peach halves and spoon the sauce over the top. Serve with mashed potato.

Serves 6–8

1.2 kg piece organic bacon, rind on
250 ml dry sherry
150 ml sherry vinegar
1 lemon, juiced
4 tablespoons olive oil
½ cup honey
75 g fresh ginger, julienned
6 cloves garlic, finely chopped
6 golden shallots, sliced
1 cinnamon stick
150 g dried cherries or cranberries
500 ml chicken stock (see page 134)
3 large firm yellow peaches, halved and
    stone removed

Eight-hour hunter's shin of beef

The long cooking time results in melt-in-the-mouth beef. Enjoy it with that favourite bottle of red you've been saving for winter.

Preheat the oven to 120°C. Place the olive oil, thyme, oregano, onion and garlic in a large ovenproof dish with a lid. Stir to coat the onion and herbs with oil, then place the beef on top and season well with salt and pepper. Add half the butter, then pour in the chianti (the liquid should cover the meat). Seal the dish with baking paper and foil, then place the lid on securely and bake for 7–8 hours or until the beef is very tender.

Remove the beef and keep warm. Strain the cooking juices, place in a saucepan over high heat and simmer until reduced by half. Stir in the remaining butter.

Serve the beef and juices with a green salad and your choice of mashed potato, gnocchi or polenta.

Serves 4

2 tablespoons olive oil
5 sprigs thyme
5 sprigs oregano
1 brown onion, sliced
5 cloves garlic, sliced
4 pieces beef shin, about 5 cm thick
sea salt and freshly ground black pepper
80 g unsalted butter
750 ml –1 litre chianti or other dry red wine

Egg, leek and bacon pies

These pies are delicious straight from the oven – when the pastry and cheese are meltingly warm. But if you can stop yourself from eating the lot at once, pack them up for an outdoor brunch or breakfast picnic.

Preheat the oven 190°C. Grease eight large muffin tins. Cut each pastry sheet into quarters and line the muffin tins, pushing the pastry into the base of each one.

Cook the leeks in lightly salted boiling water over medium heat for 8–10 minutes or until tender. Drain and set aside.

Heat a non-stick frying pan over medium heat and cook the bacon for 3 minutes. Add the shallots and cook until the bacon is crisp. Divide the leek and bacon mixture evenly among the pies and sprinkle with goat's cheese.

Combine the egg, cream and parsley and season well. Divide evenly among the pies and bake for 25–30 minutes or until golden and cooked. Serve warm.

Makes 8

2 sheets frozen puff pastry, defrosted
2 leeks, trimmed and cut into 6 cm pieces
5 rashers bacon, chopped
2 golden shallots, chopped
160 g goat's cheese
6 free-range eggs, whisked
200 ml pouring cream
6 sprigs flat-leaf parsley, chopped
sea salt and freshly ground black pepper

Mum's Wiener schnitzel

A good schnitzel is hard to beat. I still love going home to my mother's cooking, though I've tweaked her recipe a little and made it my own. The best breadcrumbs are made from stale white bread blitzed with crusts and all.

Place the breadcrumbs, mint, parsley, garlic, salt and lemon zest in a medium bowl and toss well to combine.

Dust the veal in flour and shake to remove any excess. Dip the veal in the beaten egg, then press the crumb mixture onto both sides. Rest at room temperature for 10 minutes.

Heat the olive oil in a large frying pan over medium heat and fry the veal for 3 minutes on each side or until cooked to your liking. Drain on paper towels. Serve the schnitzels with snow pea shoots and lemon cheeks. For a more substantial meal, serve with sauteed zucchini with herbs and lemon (see page 60) or braised peas with cos lettuce and mint (see page 70).

Serves 6

4 cups freshly made breadcrumbs
3 teaspoons dried mint
1 cup flat-leaf parsley, leaves finely chopped
4 cloves garlic, finely chopped
2 teaspoons salt
1 lemon, zest finely grated
6 pieces veal (about 150 g each), flattened slightly
½ cup plain flour
3 free-range eggs, lightly beaten
200 ml olive oil
snow pea (mange-tout) shoots, to serve
lemon cheeks, to serve

Braised lamb chump chops with onion, capsicum and potato

The beauty of this dish is that it's all made in one pot. Just get it started, then leave it to cook and an hour later dinner's on the table, with lamb so tender it's almost falling off the bone. Don't leave out the red wine vinegar – it gives the lamb a delicious tang.

Season the chops with salt and pepper. Heat 2 tablespoons olive oil in a large frying pan over medium heat and cook the chops for 3 minutes each side or until brown. Remove and set aside.

Using the same pan, add the remaining oil and cook the onion, garlic, chilli and oregano for 3 minutes, then add the potatoes and cook for a further 5 minutes, stirring occasionally. Return the chops to the pan. Stir in the vinegar, then add the capsicum, tomatoes and enough water to cover the chops. Cover and simmer over low heat for 45–55 minutes or until the chops are tender and cooked. Serve with crusty bread.

Serves 4

6 lamb chump chops
sea salt and freshly ground black pepper
4 tablespoons extra virgin olive oil
2 large brown onions, sliced into rings
4 cloves garlic, sliced
1 bird's eye chilli, split
½ bunch oregano, leaves only
3 desiree potatoes, cut into chunks
4 tablespoons red wine vinegar
2 red capsicums (peppers), seeded and
   cut into 8 pieces
400 g can chopped tomatoes

Roasted scotch of organic pork with Dutch potatoes and mustard fruits

Scotch fillet of pork is a lovely cut of meat to roast – ask your butcher to roll it up with a nice long piece of skin to make beautiful crackling. Score the skin quite aggressively before rubbing in the salt mix.

Grind the sea salt, pepper and fennel seeds together and rub the spice mix into the pork skin. Leave at room temperature for an hour or so.

Preheat the oven to 220°C. Scatter the potato pieces into a large baking dish, season lightly, then drop the onion rounds in the middle. Sit the pork on top and roast for 1 hour.

Meanwhile, toss the Brussels sprouts in olive oil and season well. Roast for 20–30 minutes until tender and nicely browned.

Remove the baking dish from the oven, then baste the pork and stir the potatoes. Increase the oven temperature or turn on the grill and crisp the crackling for the last 6 minutes of cooking. Remove the pork and rest on a plate to collect the juices for about 15 minutes before carving. Return the potatoes to the oven until crispy, if necessary, then remove.

Add the sliced mustard fruits, verjuice and some of the syrup to the juices and stir to combine. Serve with the carved pork, crispy potatoes and roasted Brussels sprouts.

Serves 6

4 tablespoons sea salt flakes
1 tablespoon freshly ground black pepper
1 tablespoon fennel seeds
1.3 kg piece organic pork scotch fillet, rolled ready for roasting
5 large Dutch cream potatoes, peeled and sliced into discs
2 onions, unpeeled, sliced into thick rounds
300 g jar mustard fruits, sliced, syrup reserved
200 ml verjuice

Roasted Brussels sprouts
800 g Brussels sprouts, trimmed and bases cross-scored
extra virgin olive oil, for drizzling
sea salt and freshly ground black pepper

< Pea and ham soup

I have fond memories of coming home after a busy day, starving, and sitting straight down to a giant bowl of pea and ham soup. This one is based on my mum's recipe but I like to use a whole pork hock so there are delicious chunks of meat. Don't forget the crusty bread.

Place the pork hock in a large wide-based saucepan, cover with water and bring to the boil to just blanch the meat. Drain immediately and set aside.

Heat the olive oil in the pan over medium heat. Add the onion, garlic, carrot and celery and cook for about 8 minutes or until the vegetables are tender. Season with salt and pepper and add the hock, split peas, barley, tomatoes and herbs. Cover with 2.5–3 litres cold water and bring to the boil. Simmer for 1½ to 2 hours, stirring occasionally, until the soup has thickened.

Serves 8

1 large smoked pork hock, chopped osso buco-style
   (ask your butcher to do this)
100 ml olive oil
3 large brown onions, chopped
6 cloves garlic, chopped
4 carrots, chopped
½ bunch celery, sliced
sea salt and freshly ground black pepper
400 g split peas
150 g barley
2 large ripe tomatoes, chopped
3 bay leaves
4 sprigs thyme

Chargrilled pork escalopes with fried zucchini, mint and parsley salad and dried chilli

These quickly seared escalopes are delicious with a dollop of cold ricotta. They're great for lunch or a light dinner in summer.

Heat 1 tablespoon olive oil in a large frying pan over high heat. Add the zucchini and cook for about 2 minutes each side or until golden. Remove from the pan and drain on paper towels. Sprinkle with salt and pepper.

Preheat a chargrill pan over high heat. Cook the pork for about 2 minutes each side or until cooked to your liking.

Combine the zucchini, mint, parsley, lemon slices, remaining olive oil and a squeeze of lemon juice.

Serve the pork topped with a spoonful of ricotta. Sprinkle chilli flakes over the zucchini salad and serve on the side.

Serves 4

100 ml extra virgin olive oil
2 zucchini (courgettes), sliced lengthways
   into 4 pieces
sea salt and freshly ground black pepper
4 pork loin or round escalopes (150 g each),
   flattened to thin steaks
12 mint leaves, torn
12 flat-leaf parsley leaves, torn
1 small lemon, half finely sliced and half juiced
200 g ricotta
1½ teaspoons dried chilli flakes

Roast organic pork belly

In this recipe I serve the pork with baked apples, roast potatoes and fennel, but you could also try slow-braised silverbeet or cavolo nero (see glossary) and garlic. For best results, begin the recipe in the morning or even the night before. Don't be scared to crank up your oven – you're going for the best crackling you've ever had.

Place the pork belly in a large saucepan and cover with cold water. Add the bay leaf and 2 teaspoons salt and bring to the boil over medium heat. Simmer, covered, for 1 hour.

Drain the pork and pat dry with paper towels. Score the fat with a sharp knife while still hot. Place the pork between two trays weighted with cans and set aside for 4–5 hours or overnight in the fridge (this presses the pork flat, allowing it to roast evenly).

Grind the chilli flakes, fennel seeds, pepper and remaining salt in a mortar and pestle and rub all over the pork.

Preheat the oven to 240°C. Cut the fennel into 1 cm thick slices and place in the base of a lightly greased roasting pan. Sit the pork on the fennel. Add 200 ml water, drizzle with olive oil and roast for 15 minutes. Place the potatoes and apples around the pork and roast for 45 minutes or until the pork is cooked to your liking.

Remove the apples and potatoes from the pan, and place the pork under a preheated hot grill for 5–10 minutes or until the crackling is crisp and crunchy. Set aside to cool slightly. Cut into slices and serve warm to hot with the roasted apples, potatoes and fennel. Squeeze a little lemon over the pork, if desired.

Serves 4

1.2 kg piece organic pork belly

1 bay leaf

1½ tablespoons sea salt

2 teaspoons dried chilli flakes

1 tablespoon fennel seeds

1 tablespoon freshly ground black pepper

1 large bulb fennel, trimmed

2 tablespoons olive oil

2 large potatoes, cut into wedges, parboiled
   for 15 minutes and drained, then tossed
   in a saucepan to roughen the edges

4 apples (pink lady or royal gala) or 16 cocktail
   apples, scored around the centre

1 lemon, cut into cheeks (optional)

Moorish pork skewers with orange and smoked paprika

These pork skewers are easy to make and are a great mid-week meal. To speed things up, marinate the pork in the morning before work.

Combine the coriander, cumin and fennel seeds, paprika, garlic, saffron threads and soaking liquid, bay leaf, oregano and chilli in a blender and blend until smooth. Add the orange zest, vinegar and olive oil and blend to a paste. Coat the pork with the marinade and place in the fridge, covered, for at least 2 hours.

Thread the pork pieces onto metal skewers, then season well. Cook on a chargrill or in a frying pan over high heat for 5–8 minutes or until cooked to your liking. Serve with orange wedges and rice pilaf or boiled potatoes. Shaved fennel, orange, red onion and black olive salad (see page 38) also works well with this dish.

Serves 4

2 tablespoons coriander seeds
1½ tablespoons cumin seeds
2 tablespoons fennel seeds
1 teaspoon smoked paprika
2 cloves garlic
2 pinches of saffron threads, soaked
   in a little boiling water
1 bay leaf
2 sprigs oregano
½ teaspoon dried chilli flakes
1 orange, zested
2½ tablespoons red wine vinegar
100 ml olive oil
600 g pork fillet, cut into 2 cm cubes
sea salt and freshly ground black pepper
orange wedges, to serve

Barbecued lamb with mint, peas and fetta

Choose smaller racks of lamb and cut them yourself – the meat is always sweeter and juicier on smaller racks. Or ask the butcher for double cutlets.

Combine the oregano, salt, pepper, garlic and olive oil and coat the lamb thoroughly. Leave to marinate for at least 15 minutes.

Bring a saucepan of water to the boil and salt it so that it tastes like sea water. Drop in the broad beans and cook for 3 minutes, then drain and refresh under cold running water until just warm. Replace the water in the pan, add salt and bring to the boil. Cook the peas for 1 minute, then drain and refresh under cold running water until just warm.

Remove the outer skin from the broad beans to reveal small, bright green beans and roughly chop. Place half in a mortar and pestle with the mint, extra garlic and a little salt and pound to a rough paste. Gradually add the peas, extra virgin olive oil and remaining broad beans until you have a thick, rough paste.

Preheat a chargrill or barbecue plate and cook the cutlets for 5 minutes each side, then set aside to rest for 3 minutes. Transfer to plates, top with the broad bean paste, fetta and a squeeze of lemon juice and serve.

Serves 4

2 sprigs oregano, leaves only or 1 tablespoon dried oregano

sea salt and freshly ground black pepper

2 cloves garlic, smashed

2½ tablespoons olive oil

12 fat lamb cutlets

3 cups podded broad beans

1 cup frozen peas

6 mint sprigs, leaves roughly chopped

½ clove garlic, extra

100 ml extra virgin olive oil

100 g Greek fetta

1 lemon

Lamb and eggplant karhi curry with tomato and lime chutney

Kahri-style curries are made with yoghurt and chickpea flour, resulting in a rich, velvety soupy sauce that is enticingly fragrant while you are cooking it. It pairs beautifully with the fresh tomato chutney. The chutney also works well with seared fish.

In a large bowl whisk together the chickpea flour and water. Add the yoghurt and whisk until smooth. Set aside.

Heat 120 ml oil in a large, wide-based saucepan over medium heat and lightly brown the eggplant pieces. Remove and drain on paper towel. Add the remaining oil, then toss in the cumin, fennel, fenugreek and mustard seeds and cook for 1½ minutes. Add the onion, garlic, chilli and ginger and cook for 2 minutes, then stir in the ground spices and salt and cook for 1 minute. Add the lamb, stir over medium heat for 2 minutes, then reduce the heat to low and cook, covered, for 10 minutes.

Stir in the chopped tomatoes, eggplant and the yoghurt mixture and bring to a simmer over medium heat. Add the curry leaves (if using), then reduce the heat to low and cook, half-covered, for 55 minutes or until the meat is tender. Add a little water during cooking if the curry becomes a bit dry.

To make the chutney, combine all the ingredients in a large bowl and leave to stand at room temperature for 10 minutes before serving with the curry and steamed rice.

Serves 4–6

2 heaped teaspoons chickpea flour (besan)
600 ml water
300 g plain yoghurt
150 ml vegetable oil
2 eggplants (aubergines), stripe-peeled and cut into 6 wedges lengthways
2 heaped teaspoons cumin seeds
2 heaped teaspoons fennel seeds
2 heaped teaspoons fenugreek seeds
2 tablespoons mustard seeds
2 onions, sliced lengthways
5 cloves garlic, sliced
3 long red chillies, sliced on the diagonal
8 cm piece ginger, julienned
1 heaped teaspoon ground cumin
2 teaspoons ground turmeric
1½ teaspoons chilli powder
3 teaspoons salt flakes
900 g lamb shoulder, diced
1 cup canned chopped tomatoes
12 curry leaves (optional)

Tomato and lime chutney
3 large tomatoes, diced
2 limes, juiced
½ teaspoon dried chilli flakes
3 teaspoons brown sugar
3 teaspoons salt flakes
½ teaspoon celery seeds
½ large red onion, finely diced
4 cm piece ginger, finely diced
1 teaspoon nigella seeds

Lamb korma-style curry with dirty rice

This is lighter than the traditional lamb korma. The silverbeet adds on earthy flavour and the ground almonds thicken the curry beautifully.

Combine the garlic, chilli, ginger, coriander roots, half the coriander, salt and saffron in a blender. Add 4 tablespoons water and blend to a paste.

Place the cinnamon stick, cumin, cardamom, cloves and coriander seeds in a mortar and pestle or spice grinder and grind to a medium to fine powder.

Heat the olive oil in a large heavy-based saucepan over high heat and brown the lamb for 5 minutes. Remove the lamb from the pan. Reduce the heat to low and add the ground spice mixture. Stir for 2–3 minutes or until brown. Stir in the garlic paste and cook for 5 minutes.

Add the ground almonds, tomatoes and 900 ml water and bring to a simmer, stirring. Cook over low heat for 45 minutes.

Meanwhile, to make the dirty rice, grind the cloves in a mortar and pestle. Place the ground cloves, rice, salt, lentils and 685 ml water in a medium heavy-based saucepan and stir to combine. Bring to the boil over high heat, then reduce the heat to very low. Wrap the lid or a large dinner plate in a tea towel, then cover the saucepan to seal in the steam and cook for 11 minutes. Set aside for at least 5 minutes before serving.

Add the silverbeet to the curry and more water, if necessary, and simmer for 15 minutes. Add the broad beans and lemon juice and simmer for 1 minute. Stir in the butter, if using. Garnish with the remaining coriander leaves and serve with the dirty rice.

Serves 4–6

5 cloves garlic, roughly chopped
2 large green chillies
120 g fresh ginger
½ bunch coriander, leaves only
2 tablespoons sea salt
2 pinches of saffron threads
1 cinnamon stick
1½ teaspoons ground cumin
1 teaspoon ground cardamom
5 cloves
1 teaspoon coriander seeds
125 ml olive oil
800 g lamb leg or shoulder, diced
120 g ground almonds
4 tomatoes, coarsely chopped
½ bunch silverbeet (Swiss chard), shredded
½ cup fresh or frozen broad beans
½ lemon, juiced
100 g unsalted butter (optional)

Dirty rice with cloves and lentils
6 cloves
2 cups long-grain or basmati rice, rinsed in cold water and drained
2 pinches of sea salt
½ cup small green lentils, cooked in boiling water for 8 minutes, then drained

Roast spiced lamb with fetta and pumpkin

A tunnel-boned leg of lamb will cut the roasting time in half and make the meat so much easier to carve. Served with chickpea, silverbeet and lemon salad (see page 72), this is a more exotic version of the classic lamb roast.

Preheat the oven to 200°C and lightly oil a roasting tin.

Score the leg of lamb and push the garlic and rosemary into the meat. Rub some salt and 2½ tablespoons ras el hanout into the meat, then place in the roasting tin. Scatter the pumpkin around the lamb, drizzle with olive oil and sprinkle with the remaining ras el hanout.

Roast for 45–55 minutes, then increase the oven temperature to 220°C and roast for a further 10–15 minutes, or until the pumpkin is tender and the lamb is cooked to your liking.

Rest in a warm place for 15 minutes, then carve the meat and serve on a platter with the pumpkin, cooking juices and crumbled fetta.

Serves 6

1.2–1.4 kg leg of lamb, tunnel-boned (ask your butcher to do this)
3 cloves garlic, sliced
3 sprigs rosemary
sea salt
3 tablespoons ras el hanout (see glossary)
1 kg jap pumpkin, unpeeled, cut into wedges
2–3 tablespoons olive oil
150 g fetta, crumbled

Apple and cherry deep-dish pie

Everybody loves apple pie and the addition of dried cherries and jam makes this one outstanding. You can buy dried cherries from selected supermarkets, delis and nut shops, but if you can't find them, substitute currants or raisins. It's worth making your own pastry, and this crust doesn't require blind baking – definitely a time-saving bonus.

To make the pastry, place the flour, castor sugar, salt and lemon zest in a large food processor and process until combined. Add the butter and process until the mixture resembles coarse breadcrumbs. Add the eggs, yolks and water and process until the mixture just comes together. Turn out and knead until smooth. Wrap in plastic film and chill for about 20 minutes.

For the filling, combine the apples, lemon juice, calvados or grappa, nutmeg and 170 g castor sugar in a large bowl and rest for 15 minutes. Transfer to a large saucepan and cook over medium heat for 10–15 minutes or until the apples are tender.

Place the cherries, water and remaining castor sugar in a small saucepan over medium heat and simmer for 5 minutes. Add the cherries and juice to the apple mixture and cook for 5–8 minutes or until most of the liquid has evaporated. Stir in the zest and spread on a tray to cool for 5–10 minutes.

Preheat the oven to 190°C. Grease a 26 cm springform tin or pie dish and line the base with baking paper.

Cut the pastry into two pieces, one larger than the other. Roll out on a lightly floured surface into two circles about 1 cm thick. Press the largest one into the base of the tin, making sure it comes up the sides. Spread the base with the cherry jam and spoon in the apple mixture. Top with the remaining pastry and seal the edges. Make an apple decoration with the scraps and cut a hole in the middle of the pie to release the steam. Sprinkle with the extra castor sugar and bake for 50 minutes or until golden. Dust with icing sugar, if using, and serve with cream.

Serves 8–10

650 g plain flour
200 g castor sugar, plus 2 tablespoons extra
pinch of salt
½ lemon, zest finely grated
250 g unsalted butter, chopped
2 free-range eggs, plus 2 egg yolks
2–3 tablespoons iced water
6 tablespoons cherry jam
pure icing sugar, for dusting (optional)
pouring cream, to serve

Filling

8 granny smith apples, peeled and finely sliced
2 tablespoons lemon juice
310 ml calvados or grappa
½ teaspoon ground nutmeg
220 g castor sugar
200 g dried cherries
200 ml water
1 teaspoon finely grated lemon zest

Vanilla and lemon cheesecake with poached blueberries

Wine-poached blueberries in syrup add a little spice to this classic baked cheesecake.

Preheat the oven to 170°C. Grease a 24 cm shallow, ripple-edge loose-based tin and line with baking paper.

Process the biscuits in a food processor until the mixture resembles fine breadcrumbs. Transfer to a bowl, add the melted butter and 40 g castor sugar and stir until well combined. Press the mixture into the base of the tin and place in the fridge to chill.

Place the lemon zest, seeds scraped from the vanilla bean and the remaining castor sugar in a large food processor and process until combined. Add the flour, salt and cream cheese and process. Add the sour cream, pouring cream and vanilla essence and process until smooth. Add the eggs and lemon juice and process until smooth.

Pour the cream cheese mixture on top of the biscuit base and bake for 30 minutes. Turn off the oven and leave the cheesecake to cool in the oven for 1 hour.

For the poached blueberries, place the wine, castor sugar, water and orange zest in a medium saucepan over medium heat and bring to the boil. Simmer for 8 minutes or until syrupy. Add the blueberries, remove from the heat, remove the orange zest and allow to cool.

Dust the cheesecake with icing sugar and serve with blueberries and syrup.

Serves 8–10

125 g digestive biscuits (about 12 biscuits)
90 g unsalted butter, melted
115 g castor sugar
finely grated zest and juice of 1 lemon
½ vanilla bean, split
1 tablespoon plain flour
pinch of salt
300 g cream cheese
100 g sour cream
2½ tablespoons pouring cream
1 teaspoon vanilla essence
3 free-range eggs
pure icing sugar, to dust

Poached blueberries

125 ml red wine
100 g castor sugar
100 ml water
½ orange, zest removed with a vegetable peeler
200 g blueberries

Hot chocolate and churros

You must try this traditional Spanish hot chocolate for breakfast or on a chilly autumn afternoon . . . it's luscious. The crispy bow-shaped doughnuts are great for dunking. If you're feeling extra decadent, add a dollop of double cream to the hot chocolate just before serving.

For the churros, combine the milk, butter, sugar, salt and 100 ml water in a medium saucepan over medium heat. Bring to the boil. Add the flour and stir quickly with a wooden spoon to combine. Cook for 3–5 minutes over medium heat, stirring constantly. Spoon the mixture into a food processor, add the eggs and process until the mixture is smooth.

Heat the oil in a large deep frying pan over high heat until the oil reaches 180°C on a sugar thermometer. To cook the churros, oil a spatula, then use a large piping bag with a star nozzle to pipe a figure of eight about 6 cm long onto the blade. Slip the churros into the hot oil and cook for 4–5 minutes, turning often, until golden and cooked. Drain on paper towels. Repeat with the remaining mixture to make about eight churros. Dust with the icing sugar mixture.

To make the hot chocolate, place the chocolate in a heatproof bowl over a saucepan of simmering water and stir to melt. Combine the milk, sugar and cocoa in a separate saucepan over medium heat and bring almost to the boil. Remove from the heat, pour onto the melted chocolate and whisk until smooth. Serve hot with the churros.

Serves 4

100 ml milk
80 g unsalted butter
1½ tablespoons castor sugar
½ teaspoon salt
120 g plain flour
3 large free-range eggs, lightly beaten
1 litre vegetable oil, for deep-frying
½ cup pure icing sugar, mixed with 3 pinches of ground cinnamon

Hot chocolate
220 g good-quality dark chocolate, finely chopped
800 ml milk
2 tablespoons castor sugar
1 tablespoon cocoa powder

Pavlova with chocolate cream and balsamic cherries

There is nothing restrained about this dessert. It's a real celebration dish – perfect for Christmas.

Preheat the oven to 150°C. Using an electric mixer, whisk the egg whites until thick and glossy. Gradually whisk in the sugar until thick, glossy peaks form, then fold in the salt, vanilla, cornflour and vinegar.

Line a baking sheet with baking paper and draw a 25 cm circle on the paper. Pile the meringue mixture high within the circle, then flatten the top and smooth the sides. Bake for 1½ hours until a firm crust forms. Remove from the oven and cool completely.

Place the cherries and sugar in a large saucepan and toss to coat over high heat, then add the balsamic vinegar and cook for 4 minutes. Remove the cherries. Return the pan to the heat and simmer until the syrup has reduced by half. Pour the syrup over the cherries, add the almond essence and place in the fridge to cool.

To make the chocolate cream, melt the chocolate in a bowl over a saucepan of very hot water, then leave to cool to warm. Whip the cream until soft peaks form, then gently fold through the chocolate.

Shift the pavlova to a suitable plate and fill with the chocolate cream. Top with the cooled cherries, drizzle with the syrup and serve.

Serves 6

4 free-range egg whites
250 g castor sugar
pinch of salt
1 teaspoon vanilla essence
1 tablespoon cornflour
2 teaspoons white vinegar

Balsamic cherries
800 g cherries, pitted
200 g castor sugar
100 ml aged balsamic vinegar
2 drops of bitter almond essence

Chocolate cream
400 g dark couverture chocolate buttons
600 ml pouring cream, removed from the fridge
    so not super-cold

Raspberry toffee sauce

Here's one for the sweet tooths. This sauce is lovely with almond tart, fruit salad, rich chocolate cake, or simply drizzled over ice-cream. I also like to use it in champagne cocktails. It will keep in the fridge for at least a week.

Place the sugar in a heavy-based saucepan and add enough water to just moisten the sugar. Stir over low heat until the sugar has dissolved, then bring to the boil over high heat and boil until golden.

Place the frozen raspberries in a food processor and, with the motor running, drizzle in the hot sugar mixture. Process until smooth. Add the lemon juice and process briefly. Strain if desired. Serve warm or cold.

Makes about 3 cups

400 g castor sugar
650 g frozen raspberries
½ lemon, juiced

Strawberry granita with double cream

Granita is not the same as sorbet – it should be crunchy, sweet and icy all at the same time, and it is really easy to make at home. Buy the freshest, sweetest strawberries you can find. Recipe pictured following pages.

Combine the sugar, vanilla bean and water in a small saucepan and boil for 5 minutes. Add the basil leaves, then remove from the heat and pour into a bowl to cool. Strain when cool, discarding the solids.

Puree the strawberries and lemon juice in a blender then strain through a fine sieve. Add to the cool sugar syrup, mix well, then pour into a shallow, wide tray. Freeze for 2 hours, then remove from the freezer and drag the frozen ice crystals from the edges. Return to the freezer for about 1½ hours or until set.

Remove and smash the crystals again. Divide the cream among serving glasses, then spoon in the granita. Top with a layer of extra strawberries and serve immediately.

Serves 6

130 g castor sugar
½ vanilla bean, split
350 ml water
handful of basil leaves
400 g strawberries, hulled and sliced
1 lemon, juiced
125 ml double cream
6 large strawberries, extra, hulled and sliced

Strawberry granita with
double cream (see page 199)

Plum pudding semifreddo with caramel sauce and boozy prunes

If there's the odd slice of plum pudding left on the plate, don't eat it cold – turn it into an icy dessert. If the last crumb of pudding has gone, the caramel sauce and sozzled prunes are just as delicious with vanilla ice-cream. Alternatively, buy a pudding for the express purpose of making this semifreddo, especially if a searing hot Christmas is forecast.

Lightly oil a loaf tin or 26 cm stainless steel bowl and line with plastic film. Place the ice-cream in another bowl and allow to soften at room temperature. Crumble the pudding into the ice-cream, and stir in the macadamias. Spoon the mixture into the prepared tin or bowl, tap on the bench to remove any bubbles, then cover with plastic film and freeze for 6 hours or overnight until set.

To make the caramel sauce, combine the sugar and 3 tablespoons water in a medium saucepan and stir over medium heat until the sugar has dissolved. Bring to the boil and cook over high heat for about 8–10 minutes without stirring, until the mixture is a dark brown colour. Remove from the heat and add the remaining water (be careful, it may spit). Add the butter and stir over medium heat for 1 minute. Pour in the cream and simmer, stirring, for about 2 minutes, then remove from the heat and cool to room temperature.

For the boozy prunes, combine the sugar and water in a medium saucepan and cook over medium heat until the sugar has dissolved. Bring to the boil and simmer for 3 minutes without stirring. Add the prunes and brandy and bring to the boil. Remove from the heat and rest for 10 minutes before serving.

To serve, turn the semifreddo out of the tin or bowl and cut into slices about 1.5 cm thick. Place on chilled plates and spoon on the prunes and warmed caramel sauce.

Serves 6–8

1.5 litres good-quality vanilla ice-cream
350 g plum pudding
50 g toasted macadamias, chopped

Caramel sauce

300 g castor sugar
125 ml water
120 g unsalted butter, chopped
150 ml pouring cream

Boozy prunes

250 g castor sugar
4 tablespoons water
250 g pitted prunes, soaked in hot water for 4 hours
   or overnight, then drained
100 ml brandy

Sugared brioche with balsamic berries and crème fraîche

If you want a scrumptious dessert that's ready in a flash, here's one to try. Buttery brioche toasted with butter and sugar is delectable.

Preheat the oven to 200°C. Combine the cherries, half the balsamic vinegar and half the sugar in a medium saucepan and bring to a simmer over medium heat. Cover and cook for 2 minutes, then transfer to a bowl and cool slightly. Stir in the strawberries, raspberries and remaining balsamic vinegar.

Butter the slices of brioche, sprinkle with the remaining sugar, then toast in the oven for about 3–5 minutes or until golden. Top with the crème fraîche and spoon on the berries. Dust with icing sugar and serve.

Serves 6

2 cups pitted cherries
200 ml balsamic vinegar
200 g castor sugar
2 punnets strawberries, hulled and sliced
1 punnet raspberries
6 slices brioche, about 1.5 cm thick
100 g unsalted butter
250 g crème fraîche
pure icing sugar, for dusting

> Tiramisu

I've never met anyone who doesn't like tiramisu: coffee and cream – what's not to like? I usually serve it in individual glasses but it also looks great in a large glass bowl. If you want to, you can make it a day or two ahead.

Chill six 300 ml glasses. In a large bowl, combine the coffee, marsala, Kahlua, brandy and vanilla.

In a separate bowl, beat the egg yolks and castor sugar with an electric mixer until light and fluffy. Fold in the mascarpone. Beat the egg whites until soft peaks form, then fold into the yolk mixture.

Dust the base of the serving glasses with a little cocoa and sprinkle with some of the chocolate. Add a spoonful of the mascarpone mixture to each glass. Quickly dip the biscuits, a few at a time, into the coffee mixture and place on top of the mascarpone in a single layer (you may need to break them in half). Dust with cocoa and chocolate, then repeat the layers of mascarpone, dipped biscuits, cocoa and chocolate, finishing with the mascarpone. Leave to sit for a couple of hours in the fridge if you can, then dust with cocoa and chocolate before serving.

Serves 6

300 ml espresso coffee
3½ tablespoons marsala
1½ tablespoons Kahlua or other coffee liqueur
1½ tablespoons brandy
1½ teaspoons vanilla essence
3 free-range eggs, separated
75 g castor sugar
300 g mascarpone
20 g cocoa powder
100 g good-quality dark chocolate, grated,
   or tiny couverture pearls
150 g savoiardi biscuits

Florentine biscuits

There was always a batch of these in the pantry throughout my school years and they sustained me during study. I've spiced my mum's Florentines with glacé ginger, nutmeg and cinnamon. I like to make them with dried cranberries and lemon zest, but you can use any dried fruit.

Preheat the oven to 180°C. Line two or three baking trays with baking paper.

Combine all the ingredients except the chocolate in a large bowl and mix well.

Press 1–2 tablespoons of mixture into 7 cm biscuit or scone cutters and place on the trays. Bake for 10–12 minutes or until golden and cooked. Remove and cool on wire racks.

Spread melted chocolate on the back of each biscuit and, if you like, run a fork through the chocolate to create a swirly pattern. Leave to set. Store in an airtight container for up to 7 days.

Makes about 25

395 ml condensed milk
250 g corn flakes
150 g unsalted peanuts, coarsely chopped
100 g glacé cherries, coarsely chopped
100 g dried cranberries, coarsely chopped
60 g glacé ginger, coarsely chopped
finely grated zest of 1 lemon
½ teaspoon ground nutmeg
½ teaspoon ground cinnamon
250 g dark chocolate, melted

Chocolate brownies

Be warned: these brownies are super-rich and intense in flavour. Only true chocoholics will be able to have more than one. They'll keep in an airtight container for up to a week.

Preheat the oven to 190°C. Grease and line a 23 cm square tin with baking paper.

Break the chocolate into pieces and place in a heatproof bowl. Set the bowl over a pan of barely simmering water (don't let the bottom of the bowl touch the water) and stir occasionally until the chocolate has melted.

Combine the butter and brown sugar in a food processor and process for about 3 minutes or until the mixture is pale and fluffy. Transfer to a large bowl. Fold the eggs into the butter mixture, one at a time, mixing well after each addition. Fold in the melted chocolate.

Sift together the flour, baking powder, cocoa and salt. Fold the dry mixture and chopped nuts into the butter mixture. Pour into the tin and bake for 30–35 minutes (a cake skewer inserted into the centre won't come out clean but the brownies will set on cooling). Cool in the tin, dust with extra cocoa, then cut into squares.

Makes 16

250 g unsalted butter, softened
300 g brown sugar
3 free-range eggs
250 g dark chocolate
80 g plain flour
½ teaspoon baking powder
65 g cocoa powder, plus extra for dusting
pinch of salt
100 g pecans or walnuts, toasted and chopped

Baked peaches with ricotta and chocolate

Baking peaches brings out their flavour. The ricotta adds a delicious creaminess but you can also drizzle the peaches with cream before serving. If you prefer your fruit with less adornment, simply sprinkle halves of perfectly ripe peaches with sugar and place under a hot grill until caramelised. Serve with vanilla ice-cream or crème fraîche.

Preheat the oven to 200°C. Place the peaches, cut-side up, in a baking dish and sprinkle with the combined sugars. Add the lemon juice and 1 cup water to the dish and bake for 15–20 minutes or until the peaches are golden and starting to soften.

To make the filling, combine all the ingredients in a medium bowl. Spoon the mixture onto the peach halves, then spoon some of the juices over the fruit. Bake for 12–15 minutes or until the peaches are soft and cooked.

For the sauce, place all the ingredients in a small saucepan and bring to the boil over medium heat. Simmer for 4 minutes, then strain and cool. Spoon the sauce over the cooked peaches and serve.

Serves 4

4 large ripe yellow peaches, halved and stones removed
2 tablespoons brown sugar
2 tablespoons castor sugar
½ lemon, juiced

Filling

200 g ricotta
100 g chocolate, chopped
2 tablespoons castor sugar
finely grated zest of 1 lemon
finely grated zest of 1 orange
2 tablespoons currants, simmered in shiraz for 3 minutes, then drained

Sauce

100 ml shiraz
4 strips orange zest
100 g brown sugar
2½ tablespoons espresso coffee

Rosemary, ricotta, honey and pine nut tart

This sophisticated cheesecake is neither too heavy nor too sweet. And the pine nut topping adds a slight crunch to the creaminess.

Preheat the oven to 180°C. Grease the sides and base of a 26 cm springform tin with butter and line with breadcrumbs.

Combine the rosemary and honey in a small saucepan over medium heat. Bring to a simmer, then set aside to cool.

Process the ricotta and sugar in a large food processor until smooth. Add the eggs, one at a time, processing briefly after each addition. Add the cooled honey, yoghurt, mascarpone and lemon zest. Process until smooth.

Pour the mixture into the tin, sprinkle with pine nuts and bake for 1¼–1½ hours or until cooked. Cool to room temperature.

Warm the extra honey in a small saucepan over medium heat, then smooth over the tart to glaze. Serve warm with cream or cut into small pieces to enjoy with coffee.

Serves 6–8

butter, for greasing
100 g freshly made white breadcrumbs
2 sprigs rosemary, leaves finely chopped
100 g honey, plus 3–4 tablespoons for glazing
600 g ricotta
55 g castor sugar
5 free-range eggs
200 g thick plain yoghurt
350 g mascarpone
finely grated zest of 1 lemon
55 g pine nuts
thickened or whipped cream, to serve

Coconut macaroons

These coconut macaroons have to be the easiest biscuits in the world to make. They're perfect for kids in the kitchen, too. Using shredded coconut, instead of desiccated, will result in a moist, chewy texture.

Preheat the oven to 170°C. Line two baking trays with baking paper.

Beat the egg whites with an electric mixer until frothy. Add the cream of tartar and gradually add the sugar, beating continuously until the mixture is thick and glossy. Fold in the ground almonds, salt and vanilla essence, then fold in the coconut.

Spoon walnut-sized dollops of mixture onto the baking trays and bake for 10–12 minutes or until pale golden and cooked. Remove from the oven. When cool, sandwich together with raspberry jam and dust with icing sugar.

Makes about 25

2 large free-range egg whites
¼ teaspoon cream of tartar
90 g castor sugar
40 g ground almonds
pinch of salt
1 teaspoon vanilla essence
160 g shredded coconut
4–5 tablespoons raspberry jam
3 tablespoons pure icing sugar

Dried fruit compote

This versatile dish can be enjoyed at any time of the day and will keep for at least a week in the fridge. It makes a delicious breakfast compote with yoghurt, muesli or porridge.

Combine all the ingredients in a large saucepan and stir over low heat for 4 minutes or until the sugar has dissolved. Bring to the boil, then reduce the heat further and simmer over very low heat, partly covered, for 50–60 minutes, stirring occasionally. Keep an eye on it – if the compote gets too dry, add a little more water. Serve warm or cold.

Serves 6–8

650 g mixed dried fruit (such as apricots, pears, peaches, prunes, apples or figs)
200 g castor sugar
1.5 litres water
finely grated zest of 1 lemon
½ vanilla bean, split

Pears baked in marsala

Pears are beautiful to cook with, in both sweet or savoury recipes. They have a subtle sweetness that shines with all kinds of ingredients, and marsala and pears are a perfect match in my book. The hardest thing you'll have to do in this recipe is peel the fruit.

Preheat the oven to 180°C. Place the pears in a large baking dish and pour on the marsala. Dot with butter and sprinkle with sugar.

Cover the dish with baking paper and foil and bake, turning the pears occasionally, for about 1½ hours or until the pears are cooked through and tender.

Serve the warm pears with the pan juices and mascarpone or ice-cream.

Serves 10

10 beurre bosc pears, peeled and cored
    but with stalks intact
650 ml marsala
100 g unsalted butter
400 g castor sugar
mascarpone or good-quality vanilla ice-cream,
    to serve

Baked pears stuffed with prunes, chocolate and almonds

An ideal dinner-party dessert, this dish looks impressive but couldn't be easier to make. And it can all be done ahead of time. The poached pears will keep in their syrup in the fridge for up to a week. Try them at breakfast time, either on their own or added to a fruit compote. Recipe pictured following pages.

Combine the sugar, lemon, water and white wine in a large saucepan over high heat and bring to the boil. Add the pears, reduce the heat to low, then cover and simmer, turning the pears occasionally, for 30 minutes or until tender. Remove the pears and set aside to cool.

Preheat the oven to 220°C. Line a baking tray with baking paper.

To make the stuffing, heat the sherry in a small saucepan. When hot, add the prunes and currants. Stir, remove from the heat and set aside to soak for 15–20 minutes. Strain. Combine the melted chocolate, almonds, ginger and prune mixture, then set aside until cool.

Cut the rough shape of three pears from each pastry sheet, with an extra 3 cm all round. Spread 1 tablespoon of stuffing on each pastry pear and sit the pears on top. Transfer to the baking tray and bake for 14 minutes. Dust with icing sugar and serve with a generous scoop of vanilla ice-cream.

Serves 6

350 g castor sugar
2 slices lemon
800 ml water
400 ml white wine
6 beurre bosc pears, peeled and cored, but with stalks intact
2 sheets frozen puff pastry, defrosted
pure icing sugar, for dusting
good-quality vanilla ice-cream, to serve

Stuffing
4 tablespoons sherry
6 prunes, pitted and chopped
2 tablespoons currants
100 g good-quality dark chocolate, melted
10 g toasted flaked almonds
4 pieces glacé ginger, chopped

Baked pears stuffed with prunes,
chocolate and almonds (see page 211)

Orange and almond cake

For best results, make this cake in a large food processor –
3.5 litres is ideal. It's lovely as is, or serve it with the clotted
cream for a decadent dessert.

To make the clotted cream, place all the
ingredients in a medium saucepan and bring
to the boil over medium heat. Simmer for
15 minutes over very low heat, then pour
into a container about 3 cm deep, cover
and refrigerate for 3 hours.

Place the oranges in a large saucepan, cover
with water and simmer over medium heat for
40 minutes, adding extra water if necessary to
keep the oranges covered. Drain. When cool, cut
the oranges into quarters and remove the seeds.

Preheat the oven to 160°C. Grease and line a
26 cm round cake tin.

Blend the orange quarters (rind and pulp) in
a large food processor until smooth. Add the
eggs, ground almonds and baking powder and
process. Add the sugar and process until smooth.
Pour the mixture into the cake tin and bake for
1¼ hours or until cooked when tested with a
skewer. (If the cake starts to brown too quickly,
cover with foil and continue to cook.) Cool in
the tin.

Sprinkle with the orange blossom water, dust
with icing sugar and serve with the cardamom
clotted cream and candied orange or mandarin
slices, if using.

Serves 8

8 small oranges
12 free-range eggs
600 g ground almonds
2½ teaspoons baking powder
440 g castor sugar
orange blossom water, to serve
pure icing sugar, to serve
candied orange or mandarin slices, to serve
  (optional; see page 222).

Cardamom clotted cream
500 ml double cream (45 per cent fat)
½ teaspoon vanilla extract
2 teaspoons castor sugar
4 cardamom pods, seeds removed and crushed
  to a powder in a mortar and pestle

Mandarin ice-cream with Campari and orange granita

Something citrussy and cold is a great way to finish a rich meal. This impressive dessert takes the urgency out of entertaining as it can all be done ahead of time. You'll need an ice-cream maker for this recipe.

Place the mandarin juice in a small saucepan over high heat and boil until reduced by two-thirds. Combine the milk and cream in a small saucepan over medium heat and bring almost to a simmer. Remove from the heat and stir in the zest. Allow to infuse for about 10 minutes, then strain and discard the zest.

Whisk the egg yolks and sugar until pale and frothy. Add the milk mixture and stir to combine. Transfer to a double boiler and stir constantly for about 20 minutes or until the mixture thickens. Strain, then add the lemon juice and reduced mandarin juice and mix well. Chill the mixture in the fridge, then churn in an ice-cream maker according to the manufacturer's instructions.

To make the granita, combine the sugar and water in a medium saucepan and stir over medium heat until the sugar has dissolved. Bring to a simmer, then remove from the heat. Stir in the orange juice, Campari and lemon juice. Strain and place in a container in the freezer for 2½ hours, stirring with a fork to break up the crystals every 30 minutes until no liquid is left.

To serve, place scoops of ice-cream in chilled glasses, garnish with mandarin segments, if using, and top with granita.

Serves 6

375 ml mandarin juice (bought or freshly squeezed)
250 ml milk
250 ml pouring cream
5 mandarins, zest removed with a vegetable peeler
5 free-range egg yolks
125 g castor sugar
1 lemon, juiced
mandarin segments, to serve (optional)

Campari and orange granita
220 g castor sugar
150 ml water
600 ml orange juice (bought or freshly squeezed)
100 ml Campari
2½ tablespoons lemon juice

Mini pavlovas with cream, pineapple and caramel sauce

Hot weather calls for refreshing desserts and these little numbers are gorgeous for group gatherings. Fresh pineapple and a fruity caramel sauce give the traditional pavlova a summery makeover. Recipe pictured following pages.

Preheat the oven to 140°C. Line two baking trays with baking paper.

Whisk the egg whites in an electric mixer until soft peaks form. Gradually add the sugar and beat until the mixture is firm and glossy. Add the vanilla, cornflour and vinegar and beat until well combined.

Use 2 tablespoons to form an oval-shaped mound and place on the prepared baking trays. Repeat to make 20 mounds and bake for about 40–45 minutes or until the meringues are firm. Remove from the oven and cool.

To make the caramel sauce, combine the sugar and water in a medium saucepan and stir over low heat until the sugar has dissolved. Bring to the boil, then simmer without stirring until the mixture is a caramel colour. Remove from the heat and add the pineapple and orange juices (stir carefully as the mixture may spit).

Return to the heat and add the vanilla bean and half the passionfruit pulp. Simmer for about 5 minutes, then remove from the heat, strain and cool. Stir in the remaining passionfruit pulp.

To serve, dollop the meringues with whipped cream, dust with icing sugar, top with pineapple pieces and pour the caramel sauce over the top. Serve immediately.

Serves 10

4 large free-range egg whites
185 g castor sugar
1 teaspoon vanilla extract
1 teaspoon cornflour
1 teaspoon white vinegar
600 ml pouring cream, whipped
2 tablespoons pure icing sugar
6 × 1 cm slices pineapple, cut into thin pieces

Caramel sauce
200 g castor sugar
125 ml water
150 ml fresh pineapple juice
150 ml fresh orange juice
½ vanilla bean, split and chopped
8 passionfruit

Mini pavlovas with cream,
pineapple and caramel sauce
(see page 217)

Custard tart

This rich and creamy tart is at its best when cooked until just set and eaten warm.

To make the pastry, combine the butter, flour and sugar in a food processor and process until combined. Add the eggs, one at a time, pulsing after each addition. Turn the pastry onto a lightly floured surface, knead lightly, then wrap in plastic film and refrigerate for 1 hour.

Line a 20 cm springform tin with baking paper. Roll out the pastry between two sheets of baking paper, place gently in the tart tin and trim the edges. Chill for 30 minutes. Preheat the oven to 200°C.

Line the pastry case with baking paper and fill with baking beads or rice. Blind-bake for 15–20 minutes or until the pastry is dry and slightly golden at the edges. Reduce the oven temperature to 180°C.

For the filling, place the cornflour and sugar in a bowl and stir in the cream. In a separate bowl, beat the eggs and yolks, then add to the sugar mixture with the vanilla essence and stir well. Pour the filling into the tart shell, sprinkle with nutmeg and bake for 40–50 minutes or until just set.

Allow the tart to cool and dust the rim with icing sugar, if using. (For a decorative edge, cut a circle a little smaller than the tart from a sheet of baking paper, place over the tart, then dust with icing sugar.) Serve with thickened cream.

Serves 10–12

1 tablespoon cornflour
265 g castor sugar
600 ml pouring cream
6 free-range eggs, plus 2 egg yolks
1 teaspoon vanilla essence
grated nutmeg
pure icing sugar (optional), to serve
thickened cream, to serve

Pastry
130 g unsalted butter, cubed
260 g plain flour
130 g castor sugar
2 free-range eggs

Sourdough toast with ricotta and confit orange slices

The confit orange slices take a little extra time but I promise that it's worth it. They will keep in the fridge in their syrup for four weeks.

White peaches with champagne and ice-cream

Choose your peaches carefully for this dessert – look for ripe, unbruised ones. And use the best-quality champagne and ice-cream you can get your hands on. Serve any leftover champagne with the peaches.

Place the sugar, vanilla bean and 750 ml water in a medium saucepan and bring to the boil over medium heat. Stir until the sugar has dissolved, then reduce the heat to low and add the orange slices. Simmer, partially covered, for 1–1¼ hours or until the oranges are glacéed and the syrup is thick and reduced.

Toast the bread and spread generously with ricotta. Top with warm orange slices and syrup.

Serves 4

150 g castor sugar

½ vanilla bean, split

2 large navel oranges, unpeeled and
   cut into 5 mm slices

1 loaf sourdough bread, cut into long slices

200 g ricotta

Halve the peaches and remove the stones. Cut each half into about 8 slices (or more, if desired) and arrange in serving dishes. Sprinkle the peaches with rosewater, if using, and dust with icing sugar.

Place a scoop of ice-cream on the peaches, then pour on some chilled champagne and serve immediately.

Serves 6

6 ripe white peaches

few drops of rosewater (optional)

120 g pure icing sugar

6 scoops good-quality vanilla ice-cream

1 bottle champagne or sparkling wine

Mango and passionfruit clafoutis with lime coconut cream

This dessert is light, easy and has serious wow factor. You can make it with almost any fruit – try banana or pineapple. For the lime coconut cream, you need two cans of coconut milk that have settled so that the cream separates from the milk. If you can't separate the solids, just use 250 ml coconut milk. The sauce will be thinner but just as delicious.

Preheat the oven to 200°C. Divide the mango evenly among six 10 cm ovenproof dishes. Spoon the pulp from the passionfruit over the mangoes.

Place the cream, milk, sugar, eggs, flour, vanilla and orange flower water in a food processor and process until smooth. Pour the cream mixture over the fruit and bake for 20–25 minutes or until golden. Leave for 5 minutes, then top with the extra passionfruit pulp and sprinkle with palm sugar.

To make the lime coconut cream, process the lime leaves and coconut cream in a blender or mortar and pestle or with a stick blender. Add the lime juice, then strain if desired.

Drizzle the lime coconut cream evenly over the clafoutis, dust with icing sugar and serve immediately with extra lime coconut cream on the side.

Serves 6

3 mangoes, sliced
4 passionfruit
200 ml thick cream
200 ml milk
50 g castor sugar
4 free-range eggs
80 g plain flour
½ teaspoon vanilla extract
½ teaspoon orange blossom water
3 passionfruit, extra
100 g palm sugar, grated
pure icing sugar, to serve

Lime coconut cream

2 kaffir lime leaves, very finely sliced
250 ml thick coconut cream (use the cream from the top of two 400 ml cans of coconut milk – do not shake the cans)
1 lime, juiced

Sticky date pudding with caramel sauce

Yes, the world does need another recipe for sticky date pudding, and this old favourite is a cinch to make. Served warm out of the oven, you'll find it wickedly addictive, especially with a good dollop of cream or ice-cream.

Preheat the oven to 180°C. Combine the dates and water in a small saucepan over medium heat and cook for 5–8 minutes or until the dates are very soft. Stir in the bicarbonate of soda, then set aside to cool.

Beat the butter and sugar in a bowl with an electric mixer until thick and pale, then add the eggs one at a time, beating well after each addition. Fold in the vanilla, date mixture and then the flour. Spoon the mixture into a large 5 cm deep round ceramic baking dish or a 25 cm × 35 cm rectangular baking dish and bake for 20–25 minutes or until springy to the touch.

To make the caramel sauce, combine all the ingredients in a small saucepan and stir over medium heat until boiling. Simmer for about 2 minutes or until combined and glossy.

Serve the pudding warm with vanilla ice-cream or cream and drizzle with the caramel sauce.

Serves 6–8

225 g dates, pitted and chopped
450 ml water
1 teaspoon bicarbonate of soda
90 g soft unsalted butter
225 g castor sugar
3 free-range eggs
1 teaspoon vanilla extract
225 g self-raising flour, sifted
vanilla ice-cream or cream, to serve

Caramel sauce
150 g brown sugar
250 ml pouring cream
200 g unsalted butter, chopped

Honey filo pastry layers with orange blossom cream and poached apricots

Filo pastry becomes flaky and delicate when baked with honey and sugar, and the fragrant orange blossom cream will whisk you off to a balmy Moroccan afternoon.

For the orange blossom cream, soak the gelatine in cold water until soft. Squeeze to remove any excess water. Whisk the egg, yolks and sugar in the top of a double boiler or a heatproof bowl over a saucepan of simmering water for 3–5 minutes or until thick and frothy. Remove from the heat and stir in the orange blossom water and gelatine. Fold in the cream and place in the fridge, covered, for 2–3 hours.

Preheat the oven to 200°C. Grease two or three baking trays. Place one sheet of pastry on the workbench and brush with butter, then sprinkle with a little sugar. Place another sheet on top, brush with butter, then sprinkle with sugar. Repeat to make four layers, then cut into three strips lengthways. Cut each strip into four diamonds and transfer to the baking trays. Repeat to make 24 diamonds. Drizzle each with a little honey and bake for 6–8 minutes or until golden and cooked.

To make the poached apricots, combine the sugar, vanilla bean and 200 ml water in a large saucepan. Bring to the boil, stirring, over low heat until the sugar has dissolved. Add the apricots and simmer, partially covered, for 5–10 minutes (depending on ripeness) or until tender. Remove the apricots and set aside to cool.

To serve, place a pastry diamond on each plate, then top each with a dollop of cream and half an apricot. Place another diamond on top, add a little more cream and half an apricot and finish with a diamond. Dust with icing sugar.

Serves 8

185 g filo pastry
melted butter, for brushing
150 g castor sugar
100 g honey
pure icing sugar, for dusting

Poached apricots
1 cup castor sugar
1 vanilla bean, split
8 very large apricots, halved and stones removed

Orange blossom cream
1 sheet gold-strength gelatine (see glossary)
1 free-range egg, plus 2 egg yolks
3 tablespoons castor sugar
1 teaspoon orange blossom water
300 ml pouring cream, lightly whipped

Mille-feuille with rosewater crème pâtissière and roasted berry salad

With its beautiful red and cream hues, this dreamy dish makes an impressive dessert for Christmas or other special occasions. Assemble it at the last minute because it won't sit for long in this gorgeous state.

Preheat the oven to 220°C. Place the pastry sheets on lightly greased baking trays and bake for 7 minutes. Place a heavy tray on the pastries to press down and cook for a further 3 minutes. Cool on racks, then cut each into six triangles. Reduce the oven temperature to 190°C.

For the crème pâtissière, place the milk, butter and vanilla bean in a medium saucepan over high heat. Bring almost to the boil, then remove from the heat. Combine the egg yolks, sugar and cornflour in a large bowl, then gradually whisk the hot milk into the egg yolk mixture. Return the mixture to the saucepan and simmer over very low heat, stirring constantly, for about 5 minutes or until thick and glossy. Pour into a bowl, remove the vanilla bean, stir in the rosewater and cover the surface with plastic film to prevent a skin forming. Place in the fridge to cool. When cold, fold in the cream.

Combine the cherries, rhubarb, raspberries or strawberries, vanilla beans and sugar in an ovenproof dish. Set aside for 15 minutes, then bake for 20–25 minutes or until the rhubarb is tender. Set aside to cool.

To assemble, dust the pastry triangles with icing sugar. Place one triangle on each serving plate, top with a dollop of crème pâtissière and some roasted fruit. Add another pastry triangle, a spoonful of crème pâtissière, more fruit, then top with a pastry triangle. Spoon a little of the fruit syrup around the plate and top with tufts of fairy floss, if using.

Serves 8

4 sheets frozen puff pastry, defrosted or 500 g puff pastry sheets bought from a bakery

Crème pâtissière
500 ml milk
30 g unsalted butter
1 vanilla bean, split
4 free-range egg yolks
80 g castor sugar
50 g cornflour
2 teaspoons rosewater
150 ml pouring cream, whipped

Roasted berry salad
400 g cherries, pitted
2 bunches rhubarb, trimmed and sliced
125 g raspberries or strawberries
2 vanilla beans, quartered
350 g castor sugar
pure icing sugar, to serve
Iranian fairy floss, to serve (optional; available from specialty delicatessens and food halls)

Cinnamon doughnuts with chocolate and cardamom custard

The doughnut dough will keep for a couple of days in the fridge. If you don't have time to make the custard, these pillow-shaped cinnamon-dusted doughnuts make a fabulous snack on their own.

For the custard, combine the milk, butter, 50 g sugar, lemon zest and vanilla bean in a medium saucepan over medium heat and cook until almost boiling. Pour over the chocolate buttons and stir until smooth.

Place the egg yolks and remaining sugar in a bowl and beat until thick. Add the cornflour, cardamom and cocoa powder and stir well. Add the chocolate milk to the egg mixture in three batches, mixing well between additions. Pour the mixture into a large saucepan and stir constantly over low heat until boiling, then reduce the heat to very low and cook for 5 minutes, stirring frequently. Add the almond essence, then pour into a shallow dish, cover and chill.

To make the doughnuts, combine the yeast, water and a pinch of sugar in a small bowl and whisk to combine. Place the milk in a saucepan over medium heat and bring almost to the boil, then remove from the heat. Place the butter, salt and remaining sugar in a large bowl and pour in the hot milk. Whisk until all the ingredients have dissolved, then set aside to cool. When cool, add the yeast mixture and eggs, and stir in the flour until the mixture is smooth. Cover and rest at room temperature for 1 hour.

Heat the oil to 170°C in a deep-fryer or large saucepan and deep-fry tablespoons of the doughnut mixture until golden and cooked through. Drain on paper towels.

Beat the custard and whipped cream in an electric mixer using the paddle attachment, or beat with a wooden spoon until smooth.

Combine the icing sugar and ground cinnamon and dust over the doughnuts. Spoon or pipe the custard onto plates, top with the doughnuts and serve.

Serves 6–8

1 teaspoon dried yeast
4 tablespoons warm water
50 g castor sugar
400 ml milk
60 g unsalted butter
pinch of salt
3 free-range eggs, lightly beaten
580 g plain flour
vegetable oil, for deep-frying
150 ml whipped cream
½ cup pure icing sugar
1½ teaspoons ground cinnamon

Chocolate and cardamom custard
1 litre milk
50 g unsalted butter
200 g castor sugar
finely grated zest of 1 lemon
½ vanilla bean, split
200 g chocolate buttons
8 free-range egg yolks
100 g cornflour
2 teaspoons ground cardamom
2 tablespoons cocoa powder
2 drops of almond essence

Chestnut flour and honey rosemary cake with pine nuts

This is my version of a traditional Tuscan cake with a flavour somewhere between sweet and savoury – I have sweetened mine with honey and brown sugar. Serve it with honey liqueur or mint tea.

Preheat the oven to 170°C. Line a 20 cm × 30 cm cake tin with baking paper.

Mix the flours, salt and cold butter in a food processor until the mixture resembles fine breadcrumbs. Add the brown sugar and process until combined.

In a bowl, whisk together the bicarbonate of soda, milk, water, egg, egg yolk and honey. Add half the rosemary to the bowl along with the raisins. Fold through the flour mixture, then pour the batter into the tin. Scatter the pine nuts, remaining rosemary and orange zest over the top, drizzle with the oil and bake for 40 minutes, or until a skewer comes out clean. Check the cake halfway through the cooking time and cover with foil if it's getting a bit dark.

Remove the cake from the oven and leave to cool completely in the tin. Serve as it is, or with a smear of mascarpone or crème fraîche.

Serves 10

220 g chestnut flour
80 g self-raising flour
2 teaspoons salt
185 g cold unsalted butter
160 g brown sugar
1½ teaspoons bicarbonate of soda
185 ml milk
185 ml water
1 free-range egg, plus 1 egg yolk
4 tablespoons floral honey
1 sprig rosemary, leaves finely chopped
80 g golden raisins, plumped in hot water
30 g pine nuts
finely grated zest of ½ orange
2 tablespoons olive oil

Baklava fingers

I've been addicted to these Middle Eastern pastries since I was very young. They will improve with time as they soak up all the sticky syrup. They're delicious just as they are with strong coffee or mint tea, or serve as a dessert dish with vanilla or cinnamon ice-cream.

Preheat the oven to 200°C. Line two or three baking trays with baking paper.

For the syrup, place all the ingredients in a small saucepan over medium heat and stir for 10 minutes or until the sugar has dissolved. Remove and strain, then leave to cool to room temperature.

Spread out the nuts on a lined baking tray and bake for 6–8 minutes or until golden. Reduce the oven temperature to 180°C.

Place the nuts, sugars, cinnamon and allspice in a food processor and process until the nuts are coarsely chopped. Transfer to a bowl and add the figs.

Place one sheet of filo pastry on a workbench and brush with melted butter. Repeat with two more layers, brushing each with butter. Cut the pastry in half and brush the long edges with egg. Sprinkle about 3 tablespoons nut mixture over each pastry segment, leaving a border around the edge. Roll up tightly, folding in the edges to make a log.

Brush the edge of the pastry with egg to seal, then place on the lined baking trays and brush the tops with butter. Repeat with the remaining nut mixture and pastry to make about 12 logs. Bake for 18–20 minutes or until golden.

Allow to cool, then cut the logs on an angle into three or four pieces and place on a platter. Drench with syrup and rest for 2–3 hours before serving. Baklava fingers will keep in an airtight container for up to 4 days.

Makes about 36 pieces

1½ cups walnuts
½ cup almonds
50 g brown sugar
50 g castor sugar
2 teaspoons ground cinnamon
2 teaspoons allspice
8 large dried Turkish figs
   or other dried figs, chopped
375 g filo pastry
200 g unsalted butter, melted
1 free-range egg, lightly beaten

Syrup
200 ml water
300 g sugar
3 tablespoons honey
3 cinnamon sticks
1 lemon, juiced and zest removed
   with a vegetable peeler
1 orange, juiced and zest removed
   with a vegetable peeler

Strawberry crepes with hot chocolate sauce

Strawberry crepes are a classic. I like to serve them with lemon ricotta and drizzled with this decadent chocolate sauce.

Whisk the eggs in a medium bowl. Place the butter and milk in a bowl and stir until the butter has melted. Add the milk mixture to the eggs and stir well. Sift the sugar, flour and salt into a medium bowl. Make a well in the centre, then add the egg mixture and stir until smooth, adding more milk if needed. Cover with plastic film and refrigerate for 1 hour.

Heat a knob of butter in a crepe pan or non-stick frying pan over low heat. Add a ladle of batter to the pan, and swirl to coat. Cook for 1 minute, then flip over and cook the other side until golden. Remove from the pan and cover to keep warm. Repeat with the remaining batter to make 10–12 crepes, greasing the pan with butter as necessary.

For the chocolate sauce, place the chocolate, cream and honey in a medium saucepan over low heat. Stir for 5 minutes or until smooth and glossy. Whisk the water and cocoa in a small bowl until smooth. Add the cocoa mixture and vanilla to the chocolate mixture and stir for 2 minutes. Remove from the heat, add the butter and stir until smooth.

Preheat the oven to 180°C.

To make the filling, mix the ricotta, lemon juice, zest and sugar until smooth. Sprinkle the strawberries with icing sugar and extra lemon juice. Spread about 1 tablespoon ricotta mixture on each crepe, leaving a 1.5 cm border. Place the strawberries on the ricotta with the points facing towards the edge, then fold the crepes into quarters.

Place the crepes on a lined or non-stick baking tray and warm in the oven for 2 minutes. Sprinkle with icing sugar and drizzle with chocolate sauce.

Serves 10–12

3 free-range eggs
60 g unsalted butter, chopped
360 ml milk, warmed
50 g castor sugar
220 g plain flour
pinch of salt
extra butter, for greasing

Chocolate sauce
400 g chocolate, chopped
200 ml pouring cream
120 g honey
150 ml water
50 g cocoa powder
1 teaspoon vanilla extract
50 g unsalted butter

Filling
300 g ricotta
½ lemon, juiced and zest finely grated
90 g castor (superfine) sugar
2 punnets strawberries, hulled and sliced
100 g pure icing sugar, sifted,
    plus extra for dusting
½ lemon, juiced, extra

Honey panna cotta with sesame tuille

The creamy, velvety texture of panna cotta matches beautifully with the gentle heat and aroma of ginger and the light, crisp tuille biscuits.

For the sesame tuilles, process the butter and sugar in a food processor until combined. Transfer to a bowl and stir in the egg whites, one at a time. Fold in the flour until the mixture is smooth. Cover and allow to rest in the fridge for 30 minutes. Preheat the oven to 180°C.

Make two tuilles at a time. Place 1 tablespoon of mixture per tuille on a lined baking tray to make circles about 12 cm across. Sprinkle each with sesame seeds and bake for 8–10 minutes or until pale golden around the edges. When cool enough to handle, scrunch the biscuits gently in your hand, bend up the edges and hold for a minute until set. Repeat with the remaining mixture to make at least six tuilles.

To make the panna cotta, soak the gelatine leaves in cold water. Place the milk, cream, sugar, honey and vanilla bean and seeds in a medium saucepan. Stir over low heat until the sugar has dissolved. Bring almost to the boil, then remove from the heat. Squeeze the water from the gelatine, add to the milk mixture and stir until dissolved. Strain the mixture and pour into six 100 ml glasses. Cover with plastic film and chill in the fridge until set.

Dust the panna cotta with icing sugar, top with ginger and serve with the tuille.

Serves 6

2 x 5 g gold-strength gelatine leaves (see glossary)
185 ml milk
375 ml pouring cream
50 g castor sugar
2 tablespoons honey
1 vanilla bean, split and seeds scraped
pure icing sugar, for dusting
8 pieces crystallised ginger (or ginger in syrup), chopped

Sesame tuille

95 g unsalted butter, chopped
⅔ cup castor sugar
3 large free-range egg whites
⅔ cup plain flour, sifted
½ cup sesame seeds

Choux puffs with ice-cream and hot honey-chocolate sauce

This is one of my best-selling desserts. The choux puffs freeze well (just pop them in a hot oven for 5 minutes or so to crisp them up) and the chocolate sauce will keep in the fridge for two weeks. So wonderful to know that dessert is only a few minutes away.

To make the honey-chocolate sauce, place the chocolate, cream and honey in a small saucepan over low heat and stir until smooth. Place the cocoa powder and water in a bowl and stir until smooth. Add the cocoa to the chocolate mixture and stir constantly until almost boiling. Remove from the heat, add the butter and vanilla essence and stir until smooth.

Preheat the oven to 230°C. Line two or three baking trays with baking paper.

To make the choux puffs, combine the water, milk, butter, sugar and salt in a saucepan over medium heat and stir until boiling. Add the flour and stir quickly with a wooden spoon over low heat for about 5–8 minutes or until the mixture leaves the sides of the pan. Transfer to an electric mixer and, using the paddle attachment, slowly add the beaten egg, mixing well. Alternatively, slowly add the egg and stir with a wooden spoon until the mixture is smooth and elastic. Use immediately or cover and refrigerate.

Place tablespoons of the mixture on the baking trays and bake for 6–8 minutes or until puffed, then reduce the temperature to 185°C and bake for a further 15 minutes or until cooked inside.

To serve, cut the choux puffs in half and place a scoop of vanilla ice-cream in the centre. Replace the tops and pour hot honey-chocolate sauce over the top. Scatter with coffee beans, if using, and serve immediately.

Serves 6–8

100 ml water
100 ml milk
80 g unsalted butter
1 teaspoon castor sugar
1 teaspoon salt
120 g plain flour
3 free-range eggs, lightly beaten
6–8 large scoops of vanilla ice-cream
coffee beans, to serve (optional)

Honey-chocolate sauce
200 g dark chocolate
100 ml pouring cream
3 tablespoons honey
25 g cocoa powder
4 tablespoons water
25 g unsalted butter, chopped
½ teaspoon vanilla essence

Black fig and ginger jam

I like to make a batch of jam at least once a year and this time, it's fig and ginger. Young ginger is so delicate and tender to cook with – perfect for jam.

Before you start, sterilise your jars and lids in the dishwasher on the hottest temperature, or wash thoroughly in hot, soapy water, then place in a cold oven, turn the heat to very low and leave for 30 minutes.

Combine the figs and 100 ml water in a large heavy-based saucepan over medium heat and bring to the boil. Add the sugar, ginger and lemon juice and stir until the sugar has dissolved. Boil, uncovered and without stirring, for 25–35 minutes or until a teaspoon of the mixture gels when placed on a chilled saucer. Alternatively, cook until the temperature reaches 105–106°C on a sugar thermometer. When the jam is at gelling stage, skim the surface if necessary.

Pour the jam into hot, sterilised jars. Fill the jars right to the top as the jam will shrink on cooling. When cold, seal the jars and store in a cool, dark place.

Makes about 4 cups

1 kg ripe black figs, stems removed and sliced
1 kg castor sugar
45 g young ginger, very finely sliced
1 large lemon, juiced

> Pot-roasted rhubarb

When buying rhubarb, make sure you choose thick, dark red stalks. The deeper the colour, the more intense the flavour when cooked. And make sure you don't scrimp on the sugar – there's nothing worse than tart rhubarb.

Trim the rhubarb, cut into thick slices on the diagonal and place in the base of a large ceramic ovenproof dish. Combine the sugar, lemon zest and vanilla bean and sprinkle over the rhubarb. Set aside for at least 20 minutes. Preheat the oven to 180°C.

Bake for 25–30 minutes or until cooked. Add the raspberries in the last 10 minutes of cooking. Remove the zest if you like, and allow to cool before serving.

Serves 6

10 stalks rhubarb
300 g castor sugar
½ lemon, zest removed with a vegetable peeler
1 vanilla bean, sliced very finely
½ cup raspberries

Glossary

Baharat *is a traditional Turkish spice blend that combines pepper with any or all of the following: paprika, cumin, coriander, cinnamon, cloves, cardamom, star anise and nutmeg. It is available from supermarkets and Middle Eastern shops.*

Banana capsicums *are mild-flavoured, yellow–green capsicums in the shape of overgrown chillies.*

Burghul *is cracked wheat and comes in many grades, from fine to coarse. The wheat is boiled, then dried and ground to become burghul. It is readily available from supermarkets and Middle Eastern shops.*

Cavolo nero *grows in long dark-green stalks and can be picked very young and eaten raw in well-dressed salads, or picked later and cooked as a vegetable. It has a cabbage-like flavour and is also known as Tuscan kale.*

Cottonseed oil *is a flavourless vegetable oil that remains stable under high temperatures, making it particularly well suited for frying.*

Dukkah *is an Egyptian blend of roasted hazelnuts, toasted sesame seeds, cumin seeds, coriander seeds, salt and black pepper. I love to use it in the same way as za'atar.*

Fontina *is a semi-soft cow's milk cheese with a sweet, delicate flavour. Along with parmesan, it is one of the best cooking or melting cheeses.*

Fromage frais *and goat's curd are cheeses made from fresh, uncooked and unsalted curd. They have a short shelf-life, but their unique flavour and texture cannot be replaced with a cooked milk cheese. They are available at good cheese providores and delicatessens, but if you can't find them, use a fresh ricotta or soft fetta instead.*

Gelatine *is a neutral material used to 'set' foods. Available in powder and sheet form (I use sheets), gelatine comes in varying strengths, graded as bronze, silver and gold. I use Alba gold leaf or Gelita gold leaf (both weigh 10 g for six sheets).*

Goat's curd
see fromage frais

Gorgonzola *is a cow's milk blue-veined cheese named after its place of origin, an area that is now part of the eastern suburbs of Milan. The veins are formed by pricking the cheese with long needles to expose the interior, which enables mould to form. Gorgonzola Piccante is an aged version that is slightly sharper and more intense than the younger cheese, Gorgonzola Dolce.*

Grana padano *is a younger and cheaper form of parmesan cheese. It has a sweeter, less sharp flavour so use it generously.*

Orange blossom water *is water that has been infused with an extract of the blossom of orange trees. A heady, intense liquid commonly used in salads and desserts, and refreshing in cold lemon drinks and teas, it is available from specialist food stores and Middle Eastern and Greek delis.*

Palm sugar, *also known as jaggery, is a sugar obtained from the sap of palm trees. I buy mine in a light- to dark-brown block and grate it as required, using the coarse side of a grater.*

Pancetta *is an Italian-style bacon. It is salt-cured pork belly, rolled tightly or curved flat, and sometimes spiced with dry chilli. Quality pancetta can be eaten like salami, sliced thickly for braises or thinly sliced and grilled to be eaten crisp in salads and soups.*

Pecorino *is a hard sheep's milk cheese (although cow's milk is sometimes added), produced in central and southern Italy. There are several different types of pecorino, each with its own regional accent. My favourite is Pecorino Romano.*

Pomegranate molasses *is a concentrated pomegranate juice that has been reduced very slowly to create a sweet–sour syrup used sparingly in dressings and marinades. It should have a honey-like consistency. It is available from specialist and Middle Eastern shops, and the brand I look for is AL-RABIH.*

Pomegranate seeds *have a fruity, sweet flavour and a tart pip. Use them fresh in salads and desserts. To extract the seeds, take a fresh promegranate and cut through the red leathery skin to the honeycomb pith, where you will find the red jewel-like glassy seeds. Scoop these out with a spoon and remove the pith and membranes.*

Porcini powder, *sometimes called 'kitchen tobacco', is used a lot in commercial kitchens. It's basically bits and pieces of dried porcini mushrooms ground into a powder. Available from specialty food stores, it's cheaper than buying whole porcini, and a couple of teaspoons will add a real depth of flavour to mushroom sauces and vegetable-based soups and braises.*

Ras el hanout *is a very special blend of spices – the name means 'spice of the house'. The recipe is usually a spice vendor's secret and may include up to thirty spices or more. A basic blend may consist of cumin, coriander, cardamom, sweet paprika, turmeric, cayenne pepper, sugar, allspice and cinnamon. It is available from specialist and Middle Eastern shops.*

Saba *is a type of sweet vinegar. This thick syrup, traditional made in southern Italy, is made by cooking the must (the unfermented juice from grapes that have been pressed to make wine) until the liquid is the consistency of honey. It is used as a condiment in dressings and drizzled over sweet and savoury food before serving. It is available from Italian and specialist food stores.*

Salt *I usually like to cook with sea salt flakes, but this is not essential. If you prefer to use table salt, you will need to use less than the quantity stated in the recipes.*

Sumac *is a powder ground from a sharp-tasting Middle Eastern berry. Sumac should always have a deep burgundy colour, and is available from spice shops, delicatessens and supermarkets.*

Taleggio *is a soft cow's milk cheese. It is high in fat, has a reddish soft rind and a sweet buttery texture, and is one of Italy's most famous cheeses. It is a popular table cheese, and is also excellent for cooking.*

Tahini *is a smooth paste made from ground white sesame seeds, with a little salt added. It is very intense, has a high oil content and will go rancid after it has been open for a couple of months. Keep it refrigerated.*

Verjuice *is made from unripened grapes, usually semillon or chardonnay. It has a more mellow flavour than lemon juice or wine vinegar, but can be used in place of these ingredients. Verjuice is available from delis and gourmet food stores.*

Za'atar *is a Middle Eastern spice blend of thyme, sesame seeds and sumac. It is available from spice shops and specialty stores. Sprinkle it over freshly cooked meats, fish or fried haloumi cheese, over pita bread with oil before toasting, or add it to extra virgin olive oil for a quick dipping sauce to serve with fresh bread.*

241

Thank you

Michael, my love, thank you for your patience, faith and support for my sometimes-crazy food ideas. I know you really would be happy to have the simplest of pasta dishes with a bit of bread, slightly earlier in the evening . . .

To Stella, my mischievous little bundle of joy, thank you for bringing such sunshine to our lives, and for making Mummy take the time to stop and smell the roses.

Thanks to Juju for the special bond you have with Stella, and for making it possible for us to shoot the photographs at home.

To Elizabeth, for your friendly ear and wisdom at times of great need!

To my wonderful family and close friends for simply being themselves. A special thank you to my in-laws, Lemonia and Arthur, for the constant supply of lemons and fresh greens.

Sincere thanks to my dedicated and gifted cooks: head chef Marissa, young cook Kym, and an especially big hug for Kylie for her constant support and humour, and for somehow managing to keep the challenging photography schedule at home (and me!) on track.

Earl Carter's photographic interpretation of my dishes is exquisite, and I have never worked with anyone more polite and professional. Thanks also to Wanda, the lady behind the man, and to Fraser, his assistant.

Perfect props and never-ending napkin options were sourced by the beautiful Anna Last – merci!

My thanks to David Band, whose professional opinion and art direction are superb, if a little unorthodox at times. Let's do it again really soon.

To Julie Gibbs, who has the most extraordinary ability to understand what I am trying to express and always encourages me to shine brightly. Your effervescent personality never seems to waiver – even when giving calm, professional guidance to a sometimes-edgy pregnant woman.

To Julie's expert team at Penguin, I thank you all for pulling together such a beautiful and exciting book. Ingrid Ohlsson took my undisciplined words and turned them into something I can be really proud of – I could not imagine a more gentle, calming soul to work with. And Rachel Carter applied a forensic precision to my recipes, ensuring they are easy to follow and a pleasure to use. To Anne-Marie Reeves, thank you for laying out the book with such care and attention to detail, making the design process both smooth and enjoyable.

Index

248

LANTERN

Published by the Penguin Group
Penguin Group (Australia)
250 Camberwell Road, Camberwell, Victoria 3124, Australia
(a division of Pearson Australia Group Pty Ltd)
Penguin Group (USA) Inc.
375 Hudson Street, New York, New York 10014, USA
Penguin Group (Canada)
90 Eglinton Avenue East, Suite 700, Toronto, Canada ON M4P 2Y3
(a division of Pearson Penguin Canada Inc.)
Penguin Books Ltd
80 Strand, London WC2R 0RL England
Penguin Ireland
25 St Stephen's Green, Dublin 2, Ireland
(a division of Penguin Books Ltd)
Penguin Books India Pvt Ltd
11 Community Centre, Panchsheel Park, New Delhi – 110 017, India
Penguin Group (NZ)
67 Apollo Drive, Rosedale, North Shore 0632, New Zealand
(a division of Pearson New Zealand Ltd)
Penguin Books (South Africa) (Pty) Ltd
24 Sturdee Avenue, Rosebank, Johannesburg 2196, South Africa

Penguin Books Ltd, Registered Offices: 80 Strand, London, WC2R 0RL, England

First published by Penguin Group (Australia), 2008

10 9 8 7 6 5 4 3 2

Design by Mahon & Band at Peoplethings © Penguin Group (Australia)
Design co-ordination and layout by Anne-Marie Reeves
Cover and internal photography by Earl Carter
Styling by Anna Last
Typeset in QuaySans and Swift by Post Pre-press Group, Brisbane, Queensland
Colour reproduction by Splitting Image Colour Studio Pty Ltd, Clayton, Victoria
Printed and bound in China by 1010 Printing International Limited

National Library of Australia
Cataloguing-in-Publication data:

Martini, Karen.
    Karen Martini cooking at home
    Includes index.

    ISBN 978 1 920989 86 6 (hbk.).

    1. Cookery. I. Title.

641.5

penguin.com.au

Thank you to the following retail outlets and stockists for their assistance
in sourcing and providing props for our photo shoot:

Sydney
Anibou (02) 9319 0655 • The Bay Tree (02) 9328 1101
Mud Australia ceramics (02) 9519 2520 • No Chintz (02) 9386 4800
Papaya (02) 9386 9980 • Wedgwood (02) 9899 2877

Melbourne
Aeria Country Floors (03) 96909292 • Blink Interiors (03) 9521 2208
Cranfields (03) 9525 2066 • Collect Home www.collecthome.com.au
Empire 111 (03) 9682 6677 • Izzy & Popo (03) 9696 1771
Husk (03) 9827 2700 • Market Import www.marketimport.com
Moss Melbourne (03) 9525 5014 • Minimax (03) 9826 0022
Sanders & King (03) 9500 1150 • Manon (03) 9686 1530 and
Manon Bis (03) 9521 1866 • Simon Johnson (03) 9826 2588
Space Furniture (03) 9426 3000 • Sunbeam (03) 9319 4999
Wheel & Barrow (03) 9500 2528